Cyprian Bridge

History of the Russian Fleet During the Reign of Peter the Great

Cyprian Bridge

History of the Russian Fleet During the Reign of Peter the Great

ISBN/EAN: 9783337295455

Printed in Europe, USA, Canada, Australia, Japan

Cover: Foto ©ninafisch / pixelio.de

More available books at **www.hansebooks.com**

HISTORY
OF
𝕿𝖍𝖊 𝕽𝖚𝖘𝖘𝖎𝖆𝖓 𝕱𝖑𝖊𝖙

DURING THE REIGN OF

PETER THE GREAT

BY
A CONTEMPORARY ENGLISHMAN
(1724)

EDITED BY
VICE-ADMIRAL CYPRIAN A. G. BRIDGE, K.C.B.

PRINTED FOR THE NAVY RECORDS SOCIETY
MDCCCXCIX

THE COUNCIL
OF THE
NAVY RECORDS SOCIETY
1898-9

PATRONS

HIS ROYAL HIGHNESS THE DUKE OF SAXE-COBURG AND GOTHA, K.G., K.T., &c.

HIS ROYAL HIGHNESS THE DUKE OF YORK, K.G., &c.

PRESIDENT
EARL SPENCER, K.G.

VICE-PRESIDENTS

FANSHAWE, ADMIRAL SIR EDWARD, G.C.B.
LYALL, SIR ALFRED C., K.C.B.
MARKHAM, SIR CLEMENTS, K.C.B., F.R.S.
NORTHBROOK, EARL OF, G.C.S.I.

COUNCILLORS

BALFOUR, LIEUT.-COL. EUSTACE.
BEDFORD, VICE-ADMIRAL SIR FREDERICK, K.C.B.
BRIDGE, VICE-ADMIRAL CYPRIAN A. G.
BURROWS, PROFESSOR MONTAGU.
CHAMBERLAIN, J. AUSTEN, M.P.
CLARKE, LIEUT.-GEN. SIR A., G.C.M.G.
CLARKE, COLONEL SIR GEORGE, K.C.M.G., F.R.S.
COLOMB, VICE-ADMIRAL P. H.
CORBETT, JULIAN S.
DASENT, JOHN R., C.B.
ELGAR, DR. FRANCIS, F.R.S.
GARDINER, S. R., D.C.L.
HAMILTON, ADMIRAL SIR R. VESEY, G.C.B.
HOSKINS, ADMIRAL SIR ANTHONY, G.C.B.
LOTHIAN, MARQUIS OF, K.T.
MARKHAM, VICE-ADMIRAL A. H.
MORRIS, MOWBRAY.
SHIPPARD, SIR SIDNEY, K.C.M.G.
SINCLAIR, W. F.
STEVENS, B. F.
TANNER, J. R.
TROWER, H. SEYMOUR.
WHARTON, REAR-ADMIRAL SIR W. J. L., K.C.B., F.R.S.
WHITE, SIR W. H., K.C.B., F.R.S.

SECRETARY
PROFESSOR J. K. LAUGHTON, King's College, London, W.C.

TREASURER
H. F. R. YORKE, C.B., Admiralty, S.W.

The COUNCIL of the NAVY RECORDS SOCIETY wish it to be distinctly understood that they are not answerable for any opinions or observations that may appear in the Society's publications. For these the responsibility rests entirely with the Editors of the several works.

INTRODUCTION

THE MS., of which the present edition—it is believed—is the first that has been printed in English, has already been published in Russian. It was translated by Count E. Poutiatine, whose property it is, and issued about two years ago. A review of the translation will be found in the 'Proceedings (No. 19) of the Anglo-Russian Literary Society,' written by the President, Mr. E. A. Cazalet, to whose courtesy the Navy Records Society owes the possibility of making it accessible to English readers. The title given to his work by the author is slightly misleading. It is really a history of Peter the Great's Baltic fleet. It does not deal with the naval transactions of an earlier part of Peter's reign, in the Sea of Azof and the Black Sea, but makes only passing allusions to them. In its present form the MS. seems to be a copy, by a clerk or professional copyist, in a style of writing common in the first quarter of the eighteenth century, of the author's original MS. There are a few apparently contemporary corrections,[1] in a somewhat rugged hand, much more

---

[1] Most, if not all, of the corrections are just those likely to be found necessary in the work of a copyist. Generally they are

likely to be that of a sea officer of the time than the regular one in which the work has reached us. There is one interpolation of considerable length (two MS. pages), which also seems in its present form to be the work of a copyist, whose handwriting differs a little from that of the transcriber of the greater part of the book, principally in the shape of certain letters and in being rather clearer. As a whole, however, the writing leaves little to be desired in the matter of clearness.

The literary style of the work resembles that of a log-book, so much so, indeed, that it is reasonable to assume that it was 'written up' as the events which it records occurred. It was completed in 1724—at page 67 of the MS. the author mentions 'the present year, 1724'—and thus its story ends a few months before the date of Peter the Great's death. Though the author describes himself merely as 'A Contemporary Englishman,' it is probable, or indeed nearly certain, that he was an officer in Peter's navy. His familiarity, not only with the proceedings of the fleet and of individual ships, but also

---

omissions made good, and are to be found on the following pages as numbered in the MS. itself: Pp. 2, 5, 11, 44, 59, 60, 61, 63, 64, 67, 68; and smaller ones on MS. pp. 10, 13, 15, 16, 26, 27, 31, 36; and three on p. 71. The corrections on MS. pp. 11 (omission rectified), 16 (number of guns), 26 (ditto), 27 ('Revell' [*sic*] added), 36 ('in line of battle' inserted), and 71 (two dates of dismissal, a name, and a date of death), are in a different hand, probably that of the author himself. The last correction on this page includes the date '1724,' and was, perhaps, added after the copying out of the original MS. had been completed.

The lower part of the leaf containing MS. pages 23, 24 has been cut off and a slip of paper pasted on in its place. In binding the MS. the margins of several leaves have been cut away, a word at the end of a line being mutilated here and there.

with minor incidents in the inner life of the body whose history he was writing, cannot be satisfactorily explained on any other supposition. He had, in an eminent degree, the gift of caution, of which a good specimen will be seen in his allusion to the campaign of devastation on the coast of Sweden in 1719. In the concluding portion of his work, where he discusses generally what may be called the naval position of Russia, he speaks with less reserve; perhaps because the earlier portion was written year by year whilst he was in the Russian service, when his MSS. would not have been secure against unfriendly inspection, whilst the rest was probably committed to paper after he had returned to his own country. Owing to his caution and to his persistent reticence about himself, it is impossible to identify him from internal evidence. The title— indeed the fact of there being a formal title to the book—would make it appear likely that it was composed with the deliberate intention of publishing it. The English reading public was interested in the Russia of the day. Nevertheless, the work is not one which would have been likely to entertain many readers. It had, as it still has, its value. That value, however, is of a technical and, so to speak, official character. Its comparative brevity and its contents would go far to justify us in awarding it a place in a particular class of 'Reports.' It is just the sort of document which a British subject, who had been employed in the naval or military service of a foreign state, might be expected to prepare for submission to his own Government on his return home. There is, however, no external evidence to support any such conclusion, and probably we shall not err greatly if we take it that the book remained in MS. because the writer could not find a publisher.

Most of those who have studied the published histories of Peter the Great, must have been struck by the almost unvarying omission of the authors to attach any permanent, or, indeed, considerable importance to his creation of a navy. It is only within literally the last few months that we have had it publicly demonstrated[1] that it 'has profoundly influenced the course of events.' Historians, no doubt, had dwelt upon Peter's strong nautical tastes and nautical occupations. These lent themselves much too easily to interesting narration to be entirely ignored ; but as to their real significance and ultimate effect, historians have been strangely inappreciative, or, at least, strangely silent. Yet, in addition to its 'profound influence on the course of events,' the establishment of an efficient naval force is the one reform or innovation in which Peter the Great's originality of conception is indisputable. The belief that all the political and administrative institutions, and much of the public sentiment, of Russia owe their origin to Peter's reforming energy, is not supported by authoritative records. We need not go so far as Waliszewski, and maintain that all that the great Tsar did was merely to put on old institutions a veneer or thin outer coating of novelty—*un travail de replâtrage et de placage, il n'est pas un travail nouveau*—but we must admit that in his quality of reformer Peter had several predecessors.

[1] By Sir George Clarke. (*Russia's Sea-power.* London : 1898.)

INTRODUCTION

The voyage of our countrymen, Richard Chancellor and his companions, to the White Sea in the middle of the sixteenth century, opened a chapter in the history of Russia of which there was no real interruption before Peter's time, and of which he supplied the continuation. Professor Alexander Brückner—one of the highest authorities on all that relates to Peter the Great—maintains that that voyage 'secured for the culture of Western Europe an entrance into Russia.' We may with but little exaggeration, perhaps without any, attribute to it an importance in its effect on the country not inferior to that of the celebrated journey of Peter himself to Holland and England. Many of the reforms and innovations, with the introduction of which that monarch is commonly credited, had followed almost as a direct consequence of the earlier voyage, and of the continuously more extended intercourse between Russia and her western neighbours. During the second half of the sixteenth century, foreign craftsmen, engineers, miners, artillerists, and officers had received employment in Russia. In the same century there were in Moscow enough English, Scotch, Dutch, and German residents to form a large community and populate a distinct quarter—the so-called 'German suburb.'

To whichever of Peter's reputed innovations we may turn, we find that it had been either attempted or suggested before his time. He engaged foreigners in his service: Feodore I. had given official employment to one hundred and fifty Dutchmen and Scotchmen, and Boris Godunof had enlisted two thousand five hundred foreigners in his army. Peter sent young

Russians abroad to be educated; Feodore I. had sent theological students to Constantinople; and Boris had sent young men of good family to complete their education at Lübeck, and even in France and England. Peter abolished the office of Patriarch, and assumed the virtual control of ecclesiastical affairs; under Ivan the Terrible had appeared the 'Book of the Hundred Chapters,' by which the affairs of the Church were regulated. Peter founded academies and superior schools; in the reign of his brother Feodore, a High School had already been established at Moscow. The municipal reforms introduced by Peter the Great were in reality copies of institutions already existing in Little Russia, which were extended to the rest of the country. Even in what may be called his nautical procedure he was not entirely without precedent to guide him. As far back as the Tsar Michael's time Dutch and English shipwrights had migrated first to Archangel, and then to Voronezh, where the building of flat-bottomed vessels became a thriving business. Alexis, Peter's father, employed some of them to build for him a craft variously described as a ship of war and as a yacht. The destruction of this vessel by the insurgent Cossacks in 1671, in Stenka Razin's revolt, is mentioned by Charnock in his 'History of Marine Architecture.' One of the shipwrights engaged in her construction was the Karsten Brant, whose name is so closely associated with Peter's first essays in ship-building. It was the same in smaller matters. Demetrius, like Peter afterwards, had his sham fights and mimic sieges. About 1670 Yury Kryshanitch published proposals for the forcible reform of the

Russian fashion in dress, of much the same sort as those afterwards adopted by Peter. Russians of distinction had worn clothes of Western pattern for some time. The celebrated beard-shaving decree made compulsory what an earlier decree of Alexis had made permissive.

In his foreign policy generally Peter was guided by principles much the same as those which for a long time had guided his predecessors. His expedition against Azof was merely an incident in the campaign against the Tartars which had been begun by Sophia. It was in another quarter, however, that he found more attractive precedents to follow. Patriotic sentiment, national self-interest, and the growing desire for further intercourse with the West, combined to indicate the reconquest of lost territory on the Baltic and access to the sea as proper objects of external activity. The country on the lower Neva had once been a possession of the Russians. They had not always been shut off from the sea. From the mouth of the Narva to that of the Siestra, the coast—though the name may not have been used—had once been Russian territory. It was on the banks of the Neva that, in 1242, Alexander Yaroslavitz had won the victory which earned for him the surname of Nevsky. To reach the sea was the object of all the wars undertaken by Peter's predecessors for two centuries. Ivan IV. had tried to establish himself in the Baltic and conquer Livonia. Michael, the first Tsar of the Romanof dynasty, had to abandon the effort; but the hope of regaining their lost territory remained in the hearts of his people. In the reign of

Alexis—father of Peter the Great—efforts to gain access to the Baltic were renewed. Alexis also had been desirous of recovering for his country the parts which had been absorbed by Lithuania.

It is no paradox to maintain that the seeming want of originality in Peter's aims and policy constitutes his highest merit as a statesman. His genius was pre-eminently practical. He had no sort of affinity with those enthusiastic and inconsiderate reformers who persist in trying to make changes, which there is little hope of effecting, simply because they might be improvements. He was a Peter the Great, and not a Joseph II. Though a great man, he was still a man; and, like other men, he made mistakes. He found, as others have found, that all precedents are not equally good guides. Where his genius shone with especial brightness was in the readiness with which he could desert one path to follow a better, and the rapidity with which he discerned the true significance of altered circumstances. Moreover, he could concentrate his powers on the pursuit of a new and more promising object. He began by seeking to expand his empire towards the south and south-east. He discovered that circumstances were more favourable to its first expansion in the opposite direction, and he turned to the other precedent set by those who had striven to regain the lost territory in the north and north-west. To acquire this and secure it when acquired, formed the main object on which his efforts in the domain of foreign policy were concentrated for twenty years.

INTRODUCTION

The general recognition of fact and possibility characterised his policy. Here we have to deal with only that department of it which was concerned with naval and maritime affairs, to give some account of which was the aim of the author of the MS. now published. Peter discerned, before the other sovereigns and statesmen of Europe, the secret of the Swedish Empire. It was not the youth and inexperience of Charles XII. that constituted the weakness of Sweden; it was that she had expanded her empire beyond all intrinsic capacity for maintaining it. It was not the years, but the character of Charles which rendered it in the highest degree unlikely that he would adopt the only policy which—even for a limited period—could ensure respect for the integrity of the Swedish dominions. In spite of the possession of some lofty qualities, he proved himself altogether incapable of seeing that conditions in Central and Eastern Europe had changed since the days of Gustavus Adolphus, and even since those of Charles X. Gustavus. The consolidation and development of Brandenburg-Prussia under the Hohenzollerns, and of 'Muscovy' under the Romanofs, had failed to impress him with their true importance. To Charles XII. Peter was no more than, half a century later to the young gallants who left Versailles for Soubise's headquarters, was 'Le petit Marquis de Brandenbourg,' known in history as Frederick the Great. On the other hand, Peter had not only discerned the weakness of Sweden, and rightly estimated the capacity of her king; with the insight of rare genius he also saw what ought to be his primary objective in the inevitable struggle and how it could be reached.

The loss or retention by Sweden of the conquests of Gustavus Adolphus was not a question of immediate urgency. Its solution would follow as a direct, if not an early result of the execution of certain strategic plans which Peter was contemplating. The immediate objective was the command of the Baltic Sea. As he has said himself, in the preface to the celebrated 'Maritime Regulations,' he turned his whole mind to the construction of a fleet. The combination of industry, energy, and persistence which he displayed in the execution of his project is inadequately characterised by the adjective 'extraordinary.' It was unprecedented, unparalleled. It was one of those very rare cases in which the enjoyment of a passionately loved amusement and the zealous discharge of a paramount duty happen to coincide. Some of his predecessors, as we have seen, had fancied that it might be a good thing to have a public vessel or two, if only on a river. Peter was the first to conceive the possibility of creating a real Navy, and making Russia a real naval power. Fragments of the story of this great performance are familiar to English readers. Nevertheless, the following attempt to introduce it briefly may be found worthy of attention.

In 1688, when he had just completed his sixteenth year, Peter was on a visit to an estate, not far from Moscow, which he had inherited from a collateral ancestor, Nikita Ivanovitch Romanof. This personage had been noted for his accessibility to Western influences, and had discarded the old Russian for the Western dress. In a corner of an 'old building in the flax-yard'—a sort of lumber-room—there lay, turned bottom upwards, a boat unlike the flat-bottomed, square-sterned craft used on the neighbouring rivers, Moskva and Yauza. It is believed that this boat had been sent from England by Queen Elizabeth, as a present to the Tsar Ivan the Terrible. It may be remarked that at this time Peter had never seen the sea. He wished, however, to try the boat at once; but it was too much in need of repair. Karsten Brant, the Dutch shipwright before mentioned, who had been brought over to Russia for the service of the Tsar Alexis, was sent for; he repaired the boat, fitted her with a mast and sail, and showed Peter how to manœuvre her on the river. The water there not being spacious enough, she was transported to a lake near Pereyaslavl. Here Brant and a companion named Kort built two or three other boats. It is from September 12, 1689, that the beginning of Peter's reign really dates. The immediate exigencies of his position, whilst expelling his sister Sophia from the throne which she had virtually occupied, and in establishing his own government, prevented an uninterrupted indulgence of the aquatic tastes, the possession of which he had so unexpectedly shown, and the strength of which diminished scarcely at all throughout his life.

In the spring of 1691 he was able to sail about on a sheet of water on his estate of Kolomensk. He did something more than amuse himself; he began serious measures for the formation of a naval force suitable for employment in the operations in the south which he was about to undertake. By the middle of 1692 a flotilla of small vessels had been constructed, by the help of skilled shipwrights engaged in Holland. With these men Peter closely associated himself, learnt to speak their language, and acquired no small practical acquaintance with their art. Impatient to test his acquirements on a wider stage, he went to Archangel in 1693, and there obtained his first experience of the sea. With his own hands he laid the keel of a large vessel at Archangel. He visited that place again in the following year, and made, to the fortress-monastery of Solovetski, a voyage during which he learnt what it was to be at sea in a gale of wind. It is significant that as early as September of that year (1694), Peter's Genevese favourite, François Le Fort, wrote of the Tsar's intention of having ships in the Baltic.

The resumption of hostilities against the Tartars in 1695 was intended less as a war against them than against their protector the Porte. The campaign was not successful, and the necessity of a naval factor in the composition of the expeditionary force was demonstrated. Peter's aquatic proclivities thus obtained early justification. For the operations which were to be renewed in 1696 a large flotilla was provided. Peter served in it as captain of a galley, and senior officer of the Van division. This time Azof was taken, and Peter formed the design of establishing a fleet on the Black Sea. The execution of this design was begun, and was carried so far that a

Russian diplomatic mission was enabled to force its way to Constantinople in a ship of war. It had to be given up in consequence of the disastrous issue of the campaign of the Pruth, to which allusion is made by the author of the MS. History has shown that the abandonment of the design was in reality but temporary. Peter was able to concentrate his efforts to form a navy on the expansion of that which had been established in the Baltic.

The story of his visits to Holland and England is too well known to need detailed repetition in this place. His occupation in the shipyards of Amsterdam and Deptford forms the basis of some of the most trite of historical anecdotes. What really attracted him to England was the importance of that country as a naval power. The immediate inducement to come over from the Netherlands was the prospect of becoming personally acquainted with people who not only built seaworthy ships, like the Dutch, but who also were so skilled in their profession that they could draft a full plan of a ship before the actual operation of building her was begun. This, as much as the manual work in which he engaged, showed the thoroughness of Peter's desire to acquire a solid knowledge of maritime affairs. 'He did not,' as he says himself, 'endure thinking long about it. He quickly set to work.' His conception of the kingly office was that 'the monarch himself should not be shamefully behind the rest of his subjects' in any department of knowledge useful to his country. The words between inverted commas are his own. The leading characteristic of Peter's statesmanship, its highly practical spirit, is revealed with exceptional clearness in his naval policy. The future of his empire depended on his ability to fashion, and to teach a non-maritime people to wield, that formidable weapon—a naval force. That he could even conceive the idea of effecting this, seems the more extraordinary when we remember that, for two centuries and a quarter, the Russians had been under the yoke of a people, if possible, less maritime than themselves—the Mongol Tartars; all traces of whose dominion were far from having disappeared.

Though less cruel in disposition than the members of the bloodthirsty group which predominated in the Reign of Terror, he was as ruthless as the worst of them in his methods of exterminating opponents. Still, he was no Jacobin fanatic to whom a *tabula rasa* seemed the most desirable of political acquisitions, preliminary to the formation of a new people and new institutions. As before suggested, Peter the Great admitted the conditions of fact and possibility. This was a passive virtue. He was conspicuously endowed with an active one —the faculty of perceiving and assuming control of great existing forces. He was a practical statesman and not a *doctrinaire*. The Russians longed for more intimate relations with the West, now that escape from Tartar subjugation had resulted in attaching them to the European instead of to the Asiatic state system. To resume in Lithuania what had once been theirs; to drive the Poles beyond what they persisted in believing to be the true Russian frontier; to regain the lost provinces on the lower Neva; to render impossible further onslaughts by the Swedes; to enter into the fruition of the benefits to be derived from traffic on the sea routes, the existence of which the Englishman, Chancellor, had revealed to them; these were amongst their most cherished desires.

The national aspirations, as it were, ran in many rills: none by itself strong enough to produce any great effect. Peter discerned the course of each. He gathered them into a single stream, the flow of which he directed himself. This capacity for recognising and controlling tendencies was not his only merit. No man understood better the laws of what may be called political physics. He knew that, to reach the mark with its energy nearly unimpaired, the force which he was directing must take the line of least resistance; that was to be found, not in the south and south-east, but in the north-west. It ran across the dominions of the Swedish king. Sweden, as A. Brückner says, had to pay the penalty—and it was a heavy one—of her assumption of the position of a *quasi* great power. Even had John Gyllenstjerna lived to carry out his attempted policy of making Sweden a maritime rather than a continental power, there was little likelihood that Charles XII. would follow it. The Swedes were essentially a maritime people. Their country, as regarded central Europe, was for all practical purposes as much an island as though it were surrounded by the sea. These obvious truths were concealed from the minds of the kings of alien descent who came to sit in the seat of the Vasas. No heavier misfortune has ever fallen on

Sweden than the elevation of the House of Zwei-Brücken to her throne. Kings of this family, finding themselves at the head of a race of seamen, neglected, or rather despised—even when reared in Sweden—the surest element in their power, and involved their country in distant continental wars. Even Charles XI., who recreated a strong navy, failed to perceive that his country could not be a great naval and a great military power at the same time. The lesson of Fehrbellin and Kioge Bay had not been understood.

What Charles Gustavus and Charles XII. could not see, and Charles XI. only imperfectly apprehended, was plain to Peter the Great. The naval weakness of Sweden in the middle of Charles XII.'s reign gave him a rare opportunity. Of this he was not slow to take advantage. Before quitting Western Europe to return home, he had engaged a large body of officers and seamen—mostly Dutch and English—for service in the fleet which he was intent on constructing. Several capable master-shipwrights also were engaged. The history of this fleet will be found in the pages of the long-secluded MS. now offered in print to the members of the Navy Records Society. The frequent reappearances of Sir John Norris in the Baltic at the head of a British force, continued till after Peter's death, indicate that the latter's naval proceedings did not pass unnoticed in this country. All the same, it is doubtful if our authorities of the day accurately appreciated the transformation effected by those proceedings in Northern Europe. Peter himself thoroughly understood the effect of his own work.

INTRODUCTION

The half worn-out boat which had attracted his boyish attention he told his companions to regard as the 'Little Grandsire of the Russian Fleet,' a title which has always been retained, for this interesting craft has been preserved down to our own days as a sacred monument of the foundation of the Russian Navy.

When Peter assumed the rank of Vice-Admiral it was with justifiable pride that he recalled what had been done. He could well 'ask his comrades whether, twenty years before, any of them ever dreamt of winning a naval battle in the Baltic, and of living in a town built on soil conquered from the enemy.'

The spelling of the MS., as was to be expected, did not need to be modernised in many places. The commonest alteration made has been the erasure of the now obsolete final 'e.' The forms 'it's' and ''em' for 'it is' and 'them' have been retained as belonging rather to style than spelling. The use of both 'Russ' and 'Russian' has been retained also, as an interesting reminder of a time of transition when the exact national appellation in English was still undecided. As regards geographical names, those of places on the coast—the majority—have been spelled as they are in *The Baltic Pilot*, and *The Norway Pilot*, published by the Hydrographer of the Navy. Well-known names like Moscow have been made to follow the usual form of the present day. Other Russian place and personal names have been transliterated from the Russian in accordance with the system adopted by the Royal Geographical Society. For Dutch personal names the spelling of the *Biographisch Woordenboek der Nederlanden* (Haarlem, 1852, 21 vols.) has been taken as the standard. The spelling of Danish personal names has been made to accord with that of the *Dansk Biografisk Lexikon*, by C. F. Bricka (Copenhagen, only 9 vols. published as yet). For Swedish personal names the guide has been *Biografiskt Lexikon öfver Namnkunnige Svenske Män* (Stockholm, 1874, 23 vols. and 9 supplementary vols.). Where it has seemed necessary the spelling of the *Dictionary of National Biography* has been followed in the case of the names of British subjects mentioned in the MS.

For the division of the MS. into sections, and for the headings to these, the Editor is responsible. He has to thank his old messmate Professor J. K. Laughton for much freely rendered assistance.

CONTENTS.

		PAGE
INTRODUCTION	. . . . . .	vii
I.	Peter the Great's early efforts to create a naval force	1
II.	First contact with the Swedes in the Baltic Sea .	7
III.	Foundation of St. Petersburg and beginning of the Russian Baltic fleet	9
IV.	Early services of the new Baltic fleet . .	15
V.	Operations in 1712	18
VI.	Operations in 1713	20
VII.	Courts-martial .	25
VIII.	Proceedings in 1714	28
IX.	The affair of Hangö Head—Defeat of the Swedes	34
X.	The Tsar's landing in a gale of wind—Arrangements made after the end of the year's campaign	39
XI.	Proceedings in 1715	41
XII.	Proceedings in 1716 . . .	45
XIII.	Operations of 1717	52
XIV.	Events in 1718	56
XV.	Naval administration and proceedings in 1719. . .	61
XVI.	Events in 1720	75
XVII.	Digression concerning General-Admiral Count Apraxin	77
XVIII.	Proceedings in 1721	80
XIX.	Digression on the relations between Admirals Gordon and Sievers	84
XX.	Arrangements for 1722 . . .	89
XXI.	An account of the galley fleet .	94
XXII.	Pay of officers and dockyard officials . .	96
XXIII.	Warrant officers and seamen .	102
XXIV	The Tsar's Baltic interests . .	106

CONTENTS

		PAGE
XXV.	Necessity of sea experience for the Tsar's Navy	108
XXVI.	The Russian Baltic fleet	109
XXVII.	Questions relating to officers	119
XXVIII.	Various works in hand—Concluding remarks	123
XXIX.	List of Russian ships in 1724	126
XXX.	List of officers in the Russian Navy in the Baltic	128
XXXI.	General list of Russian ships, 1710-1724	130

APPENDIX A. The Swedish Navy in Peter the Great's time . . 133
APPENDIX B. Englishmen and Scotchmen in the service of the Swedish Admiralty in the seventeenth and eighteenth centuries 141
APPENDIX C. The Swedish SKÄRGÅRDS fleet, or special coast service force 144
APPENDIX D. Official declarations of naval policy in Sweden . 148
APPENDIX E. Pay of the English Navy in the age of Peter the Great 149

INDEX . . . 155

THE RUSSIAN FLEET

UNDER

PETER THE GREAT

I. PETER THE GREAT'S EARLY EFFORTS TO CREATE A NAVAL FORCE.

THE Tsar[1] from his youth was a lover of shipping, and had several vessels built by Greeks and Italians, at Voronezh on the river Don, to transport ammunition, artillery, and part of the army, to the siege of Asof in 1695. He had also some galleys there, of service when the Turks attempted to throw in a relief by sea. For the Russ erecting in an island a battery unknown to the enemy, in concert with these galleys, soon mastered the Turkish vessels, and good store of gold aboard, designed for the payment of the garrison, was given by the Tsar to the soldiery. This defeat facilitated the surrender of Asof in 1696; and the taking of this

[1] 'Ayant servi primitivement à désigner les princes tartars de Kazan, ce mot [Tsar] correspond au *Sar* persan, au *Sir* anglais, et au *Sire* français avec une valeur analogue.' (*Pierre le Grand: L'Éducation—l'Homme—l'Œuvre*, by K. Waliszewski, Paris, 1897; p. 17).

place, opening a passage into the *Palus Mæotis*, first led the Tsar to entertain a thought of establishing a naval force. But having never seen any ships of war and of consequence [being] no judge, by a prepossession natural to the Russ, conceiving the builders of his galleys capable of all things bordering on their profession, he ordered them to build him ships of war. The method taken by this Prince to defray the expense, greatly enhanced through want of knowledge to make a proper estimate, was a kind of tax in nature of a benevolence, imposed on his Boyars and great men;[1] or in case of misdemeanour inflicted [as] a mulct.

Besides these preparations on the river Don; much about the same period of time, the Tsar determining to have a fleet on the Volga, travelled in person to view the course and extent of this famous river, but when [he] got as far as Sviaska, 15 miles above Kazan, the arrival of some extraordinary news obliged him to return to Moscow. However, before his travels in 1697, he gave directions to some Hollands masters for the building of near 100 vessels of burthen, chiefly designed for

[1] This method of meeting the cost of a naval establishment seems, as suggested by Professor Alexander Brückner, to have been copied from the institutions of ancient Athens. Certain classes of the population were divided into 'companies' for financial purposes, like the Athenian ναυκραρίαι; and on these companies were laid the burdensome public duties, like the λειτουργίαι, of building and equipping ships of war. An approximate estimate of the property or number of peasants belonging to the best-situated ecclesiastical and lay proprietors was made, on which it was calculated that 48 vessels could be provided. There were 17 ecclesiastical and 18 lay companies. By ukase any one who should withdraw from the performance of the public duty assigned to him was threatened with confiscation of property. (*Peter der Grosse*, by Dr. Alexander Brückner, Professor an der Universität Dorpat: Berlin, 1879; p. 342). The plan was abolished later (see p. 5). It is just possible that Peter's 'companies' were suggested by the Swedish institution mentioned in Appendix A.

trade, and occasionally for transporting an Army. Part were launched, rigged, and sent down to Astrakhan; some they since essayed to bring up the Volga, and by the channels [1] of other rivers, in conjunction with the Ladoga Lake, to St. Petersburg: but the frequent shallows rendering the design abortive the ships lie rotting near Vishni-Volochok in the road from Moscow to St. Petersburg. The remainder, about 50 in number, were to be seen last year [2] at Usleno, three leagues from Kazan, built at the same time, but never launched, on account, as supposed, of their too great bulk and drawing too much water. For the Volga, emptying itself by several mouths into the Caspian Sea, casts up sands to that degree, that four or five leagues from land they often find no more than eight foot of water, to their extreme difficulty and danger in navigation. The Tsar being the only Prince that has ships on that Sea, there is the less occasion for vessels of much burthen; *chalks* and *evers* [3] sailing with one mast, and requiring little water, plying constantly to and fro to transport passengers and merchandise betwixt Persia and Astrakhan.

Three or four snows [4] and as many yachts of ten or twelve guns apiece, have also been employed for some years past in making discoveries. All the vessels used in this Sea are built at Kazan, about

[1] Word in MS. imperfect.   [2] 1723.
[3] Ever: 'A vessel used on the Lower Elbe, mostly for passages from Hamburg to Haarburg and neighbouring places. She is sharp-ended forward and abaft, has a flat bottom, and is furnished with oars and one sail' (Zedler's *Grösses vollständiges universal Lexikon* : Leipzig and Halle; vol. viii. ; 1734 ; p. 2094).
[4] Snow, *Schnau*; Fr. *senau*; Dut. *Snaw* : 'A long swift boat used by the Flemings; but, at the most, cannot carry more than 25 men' (Zedler, vol. xxxv.). This was different from the English 'snow,' which is really a brig with a main-trysailmast and a main trysail instead of a large boom-mainsail (Burney's edition of Falconer's *Dictionary*, 1815, p. 487).

1100 miles above Astrakhan. In a word, little is to be said in favour of the ships built before the Tsar's return from his travels; to pass them by in silence is the highest compliment.

In this state stood his Navy when he travelled into England and Holland; where he gratified his natural curiosity of inspecting into the theory and practical parts of ship-building, especially in Holland, with very great assiduity; whilst others in his retinue [1] actually applied to learn the arts of mast-making, sail-making, and other trades allied to shipping. Liberty was also indulged him of engaging in his service masters in these several sciences. At his return into Russia, having quelled the rebellion of the Streletz fomented by his sister,[2] he began in earnest to new model his country: and finding himself sovereign of vast dominions, and absolute master of the lives and fortunes of innumerable subjects, without delay he set about the accomplishment of his great designs, especially those that had a tendency to promote his darling project of a Naval Power.

At this crisis Count Golovin [3] was Admiral, and

[1] MS. 'Retinew.'   [2] The Tsarevna Sophia.

[3] Feodore Alexeievitz Golovin; born 1650; died August 14, 1706. Went to China and concluded the celebrated Treaty of Nertschinsk, August 27, 1689. In 1696 Commissary-General in Scheïn's expedition against Asof. On May 1, 1699, without any knowledge of sea-affairs (*ohne etwas vom Seewesen zu verstehen*), High Admiral of the Asof fleet. 'Golovin under Peter's supervision conducted the whole policy, concluded alliances, and united in his own person the highest Civil and Military offices.' In 1700 Field-Marshal and Generalissimo against the Swedes. The title of Count was almost unknown in Russia before the time of Peter the Great, who induced the Emperor Leopold I. to create Golovin a Count of the Holy Roman Empire. Golovin was thus the first Russian on whom the title of Count was conferred. His family was, however, ancient and distinguished (*Russland's Geschichte und Politik dargestellt in der Geschichte des russischen hohen Adels*; by Dr. Arthur Kleinschmidt; Cassel, 1877; p. 168).

the present General Admiral[1] Apraxin Admiraliteitsheer,[2] so called according to the custom of Holland, and answers in some measure to the Navy Board[3] in England. Mr. Cruys, formerly Equipage Master[4] at Amsterdam, entering into the Tsar's service in the character of Vice-Admiral, entertained by his order many sea Officers; mostly Hollanders and Danes; and conducted them by the route of Archangel to Moscow and Voronezh. The Tsar justly giving the preference in building and equipping ships to the method used in England, procured several Sea-officers, Master-builders, &c., of that nation to accompany or follow him; and having now gained a competent skill in shipping, soon put a stop to the proceedings of the old builders hitherto employed on the river Don; and, abolishing the custom of enjoining his Boyars to build him ships, appropriated particular funds to that use, fixing the following persons at Taveroff and Voronezh: Messrs. Joseph Ney, Richard Cosens, and [John] Deane,[5] Master Builders; Davenport, Hadley,

[1] For an account of Apraxin, see *post*, p. 77.
[2] Calisch (*Dutch-English Dict.*), 'Lord of the Admiralty.' The MS. has 'Admiralty de's Heer.'
[3] Meaning here Admiralty.
[4] *Equipage-meester*, now 'Boatswain,' formerly meant an official like the English 'Master-Attendant,' now 'Staff-Captain,' of a dockyard. Cruys was one of the most prominent foreigners in Peter's fleet. Born at Stavanger in Norway on June 14, 1657; died on his seventieth birthday (June 14, 1727). Went to Holland when young and entered the merchant service. He was taken—as stated in the text—into the Government service as Under Equipage Master at Amsterdam dockyard. He made the acquaintance of Peter the Great during that monarch's visit to Holland in 1697, and was induced to enter the Russian Navy (Bricka's *Dansk Biografisk Lexikon*; vol. iv.; Copenhagen, 1890; pp. 118–9). See *post*, p. 61.
[5] This [John] Deane was the son of the eminent Harwich master-shipwright, Sir Anthony Deane. He accompanied Peter the Great to Russia. In 1699 John Deane published in London *A Letter from Moscow to the Marquess of Carmarthen, relating to*

Johnston, Gardiner, and Webb, Builders-Assistants; Baggs, a Master Block-maker, and Wright, a Master-Mast-maker; all Englishmen. A yard was made, storehouses and magazines provided, with houses for all men of rank according to their degree. The Tsar [was] so eager in pursuit of his purpose, that frequently visiting and sometimes residing on the spot, the work of some ships was carried on under his directions, and of those he would be accounted the builder. No cost was spared in the finishing and adorning part; and first and last were built about 30 Men of War from 80 to 40 guns, with frigates, galleys, transports, &c. In the mean time the great works of Kamishinka described by the ingenious Captain Perry;[1] the attempt to cut a communication betwixt the Don and the Volga; and the Haven of Taganrog,[2] all of fine stone, reputed second to none, went on at vast profusion of treasure and expense of the lives of men. The design of this armament, in so remote a part of his dominions, on the river Don issuing into the Palus Mæotis, must be addressed against the Turk; and primarily, at a favourable juncture, against the important fortress of Kertch,[3] commanding the

the Czar of Muscovy's forwardness for his Great Navy, Moscow, March 8, 169$\frac{7}{8}$ (see Deane, Sir Anthony, in *Dict. National Biography*, vol. xiv.).

[1] John Perry, born at Rodborough, Gloucestershire, in 1670. Entered the Navy and at the beginning of 1690 was Lieutenant of the Montagu. Lost the use of his right arm in an action with a French privateer. In 1693 commanded the Cygnet, fire-ship, for the loss of which he was tried by court-martial. Arrived in Russia in 1698, having been engaged as civil engineer at a salary of 300*l*. 'During fourteen years' service in Russia he received only one year's salary.' Returned to England in 1712. Died at Spalding in February, 1732 (*Dict. Nation. Biog.* vol. xlv.). See also *The State of Russia under the present Czar*, by Captain John Perry, London, 1716.

[2] MS. 'Tagonerode.'   [3] MS. 'Kertse.'

intercourse between the Palus Mæotis and Pontus Euxinus. But these things are mentioned, *en passant*, only to introduce an account of the Tsar's maritime achievements on the Baltic and at his beloved St. Petersburg; of more importance to be known as more immediately affecting the political interests on this side of Europe.

II. FIRST CONTACT WITH THE SWEDES IN THE BALTIC SEA.

In 1703 the Russians, after some resistance, took and razed to the ground Nyenskans, a small town and garrison, about a league higher than [St.] Petersburg now stands, disposing the inhabitants into distant parts of Russia. A squadron of Swedish ships of war arriving at the Island Retusari,[1] now Kronslot, ignorant of the fate of Nyenskans, dispatched a snow of 12, and a longboat with 4

[1] Retusari was the Finnish name of Kotlina Island (Ersch and Gruber, *Allgemeine Encyclopädie*, 40th part, Leipzig, 1886, p. 86). The author of the MS. never uses the name Kronstadt, but always Kronslot. The latter was really the name of a fort on a shoal south of the island (see *post* III.). 'A narrow streak of sea occupies the space between this island and a sandbank on which an old fort, Kronslot or Kron-schloss, commanded the only passage to St. Petersburg. With sounding lead in hand the Tsar himself examined the depth of water and the nature of the bottom, in order to carry out in the most suitable position new works for the defence of the new capital [St. Petersburg] and his future Baltic fleet.' 'Building materials had been brought over the firmly compacted ice. Immense boxes, 30 feet long, 15 broad and 10 deep, had been made and, when filled with stones, had been let down into the sea so as to form a firm foundation. . . . Opposite the castle two batteries were erected on the shores of Kotlina Island. In 1710 there first arose on the eastern part of the island the future Kronstadt, which however received the name only in 1721, being in the mean time, as well as the Castle, called Kronslot,' &c. (Herrmann, *Geschichte des russischen Staates*; Hamburg, 1849; vol. iv. pp. 160-2).

swivel guns, to enquire into the state of the garrison. About 2 miles up the river they saw the Russ army on all sides, and perceived the place was taken. However, unapprehensive of danger by water, as knowing the Russ to have no vessels of force there, they stayed a while making observations in the face of the enemy's army. The Tsar then present in person, impatient of this bravado, consulting his sea officers, ordered a detachment of chosen men and all that knew anything of the sea, well armed, to fall down the river in as many *lotkeys*[1] as they could possibly assemble in so short a space of time and wait the Swedes' return at the bar; a narrow place full of shoals, without beacons to direct the ships' course, and abounding with sandbanks on every side, proper for the reception of the Russ *lotkeys*, but incommodious to the enemy. The Swedes, observing the descent of the *lotkeys* by another branch of the river, determined to retreat to their fleet, but when they reached the bar, night coming on, and an adverse westerly wind obliging them to drive with the current, the Russians attacked them, pouring in from every quarter incessant volleys of shot. The Swedes made a brave defence, doing great execution with their guns, till at length, confounded with the obscurity of the night, contrary wind, and inequality of the fight, the snow, striking on a sandbank, was, after a desperate resistance and the death of most of the men, taken; and the long boat of course shared the same fate.[2] Immediately

---

[1] Small craft called by the Swedes *lådja* or *lodja* (plural, *-or*). In the Baltic and White Sea campaigns (1855-6) these became well known to our seamen, who used to call them 'lodgers.'

[2] The discrepancy between historians as to the date of this affair is greater than even confusion between dates O.S. and dates N.S. suffices to explain. A. Brückner (*Peter der Grosse*, p. 379) puts it 'immediately after' May 1, 1703. Schuyler (*Peter the Great*, vol. i. p. 523) gives the date as May 18, 1703. Herrmann's

upon the surrender the Tsar came aboard, and finding the mate alive that commanded the boats, ordered care to be taken of his wounds, and when healed persuaded him to enter into his service. His name is Charles van Werden, an ingenious man, since gradually advanced, and now one of the Tsar's favourite captains ; and will be farther mentioned in the sequel of this story. This was the first vessel of force the Tsar ever had on the Baltic, and though a trifle in itself, yet falling so luckily into his hands he received it as a good omen ; interpreting it a peculiar direction of Providence in favour of his maritime undertakings.

III. FOUNDATION OF ST. PETERSBURG AND BEGINNING OF THE RUSSIAN BALTIC FLEET.

Hereupon the Tsar took a resolution to build St. Petersburg. A plan was drawn and approved ; storehouses erected and a yard gradually formed, inclosed with a ditch and palisades to prevent the incursion of an enemy : Vice-Admiral Cruys with several officers and seamen from Voronezh to settle there ; and the castle or citadel, a regular fortification of 6 bastions and a crownwork, carried on by a vast number of hands, as the season of the year permitted. The Tsar also commanded a settlement to be made on the Island Retusari, in the Russ, Kotlina Ostrov,[1] now generally known by the name

date is July $\frac{1}{2}\frac{8}{0}$, 1702 (*Gesch. russ. Staates*, iv. p. 137). The Swedish naval historian P. O. Bäckström (*Svenska Flottans Historia*, Stockholm, 1884, p. 170) and his countryman Mankell (*Studier öfver Svenska Skärgårds-Flottans Historia*, Stockholm, 1855, p. 15) agree in giving July 11, 1702 as the date.

[1] *Baltic Pilot*, ii. p. 295 ; Vsévolojsky, *Dictionnaire Géographique*, &c., Moscou, 1823. The MS. has 'Cotling Oustra.' (See p. 7, note.)

of Kronslot and so termed hereafter, unless any particular incident obliges to use a distinction: though that name properly belongs to a round fortification, on a sandbank, on the other side of the principal channel for the ships' passage, half gunshot from the island. Three batteries were raised, and behind the uppermost the haven designed with a sort of fortification of turf at the west end of the island, named after Prince Menshikoff,[1] Alexander Schans.[2]

In 1705, and the following year, some frigates, none exceeding 30 guns, were launched, with several snows and vessels of burthen for service on the River. About this time two Master Builders more, Messrs. Bent and Richard Browne, arrived from England; the latter served Mr. Harding[3] that

---

[1] The celebrated favourite of Peter the Great. Alexander (Danilovitsch), son of the farmer (*bauer*, free peasant) Daniel Menshik, was born near Moscow on November 27, 1672. His father, says Kleinschmidt, put him in the service of a Moscow pastrycook, whose wares he sold in the streets. This has been denied, and the selling of pastry by the future powerful favourite has been declared to have been a mere frolic or practical joke. He entered the service of the Swiss Lefort as lackey, and attracted the notice of Peter, who made him *Denschtschik*, or Aide-de-Camp, and called him Menshikoff. He took part, in company with the Tsar, in the affair with the Swedish small craft just mentioned. His biography after this belongs to the public history of Russia. In 1705 the Emperor Leopold made him a Prince of the Holy Roman Empire. In 1707 Peter conferred on him the title of Prince of Ingermanland, with the designation of 'Serene Highness,' making him the first Russian to receive this princely dignity. He was Rear-Admiral in 1718. He died in November 1729.

[2] That is to say, 'Alexander Redoubt *or* Entrenchment.' The word in the text is the Dutch *schans*=Swedish *skans*, and our word *sconce* (Calisch, *Woordenboek*). The last is rarely used in English for fortification, though *ensconced* (=entrenched) is not uncommon.

[3] The Royal Sovereign here mentioned was, most likely, the successor of the celebrated ship which, when being prepared for rebuilding a *second* time at Chatham in January 1696, 'accidentally took fire and was totally consumed' (Derrick, *Memoirs of*

built the Royal Sovereign, and has since given the world a demonstration of his great genius that way by building the Tsar several ships, from 90 to 16 guns, that may vie with the best in Europe for the part that concerns the builder. These two gentlemen were employed on the Ladoga Lake ; for the Tsar at that time, not being master of all Carelia, had some small vessels there to annoy the enemy's fishing and commerce ; and by frequent landings destroy the villages and carry off the cattle.

When the fortifications at Kronslot were brought to a considerable state of perfection, the Russ frigates and snows used yearly to descend [the river], and lie in a half moon under cover of the artillery. The Swedish fleet would all come, can-

---

the Royal Navy, p. 64 and also p. 285). A Mr. Harding built the Boyne at Chatham in 1692 (Charnock, *Hist. Marine Archit.*, vol. ii. p. 433). Pepys had written in 1686 that Mr. Harding, assistant at Deptford, was 'a very slow man, nor ever built a ship in his life' (J. R. Tanner, in *English Histor. Review*, January 1899, p. 63). Professor Laughton has supplied me with the following minutes of a court-martial held on board the St. Michael, February 4, 1695-6 :—

'Enquiry was made into the occasion of the loss of his Majesty's ship the Royal Sovereign which was burnt at her moorings near Gillingham, in the River Medway, about 5 aclock in the morning on the 27th day of January, 1695-6 ; which matter having been strictly examined into by the Court, It appeared to the Court that the fire began in a cabin near the entering port, where an old man, one Thomas Couch, lay, who left a candle in the cabin and was himself upon deck, it being his watch. And the Court do find that he has been guilty of negligently performing his duty and it is resolved that he falls under the 27th Art. and the Court does adjudge that the said Thomas Couch shall be carried in a boat with a halter about his neck on board the hulk against Chatham dock next musterday, and there receive 31 stripes on his bare back, and that he be afterwards carried on shore and delivered to the Marshall and be imprisoned during life, and that he forfeit all the pay due to him to the chest at Chatham.' (See list of 1699 in *Nav. Rec. Soc.*, vol. v. p. 194.)

nonade, and sometimes bombard them; but never made a bold attack, deterred with the appearance of a fortification, of an orbicular form, that could bring few guns to bear. Had they once pushed in, the batteries could have done little damage, and a few single-decked ships might have easily been destroyed; the Russians expecting no less. Once they brought a good fleet of men-of-war, and a considerable number of troops in transports, attempting to land, but acted as if they had never been upon the coast before. For generally all round the island is shoal water, and uneven stony ground; but the water was deeper than ordinary betwixt the place of the Swedes' descent and the shore, taking the soldiers up to the chin, and wetting their powder and arms; whilst the Russians lying concealed in the island, then all a wilderness of trees and shrubs, observed their miserable condition; and, permitting them to gain the shore, attacked them at this disadvantage, and obliged them to return to their ships with very great slaughter. Vice-Admiral Cruys commanded in chief on the island and Colonel Nieroth[1] the Swedish troops that landed. This man, a Livonian by birth, and having an estate there, after the Tsar subdued that Province, took service under him, and was since made Vice-President of the College of War.

Another time General Lybecker[2] with a good

[1] MS. 'Nerod.'
[2] Georg Lybecker, son of Major-General Georg Henric Lybecker, Governor of Göteborg, who was ennobled in 1650. Lybecker is celebrated for his want of success. He became *Ryttmästare* (Captain of Horse) in 1682. Distinguished himself at Klissow in 1702 and in other affairs; Major-General, 1706; Baron, 1707; Lieut.-General, 1710. On February 4, 1717, he was brought before a general court-martial, and on August 13, 1717, sentenced to loss of life, honour, and goods. Pardoned by the King. Died July 4, 1718. 'Though courageous and efficient in subordinate positions, he was without the weight and skill

body of troops marched through Finland and crossed the Neva, in spite of the Russians, some leagues above St. Petersburg, designing to burn the southern part of it, on the Ingermanland side, where then were the storehouses, magazines, ships on the stocks, and the principal part of the buildings. The Russians, destitute of force to oppose this design, had recourse to stratagem, writing letters to the governors and commandants of the nearest places, to send forthwith such and such regiments, either not in being or in remote parts, to their assistance. These letters, as they intended, fell into the enemy's hands, and, striking them with a panic fear, they drew off with precipitation to Cape Karavalda,[1] five leagues below Kronslot, and there by the General's order killing all their horses, and embarking on board the Swedish Fleet, were transported to Viborg. These mistakes of the Swedes greatly encouraged the Russians, whereas, if they had taken opportunity by the forelock, the Tsar would have met with insuperable obstacles in increasing his naval power: considering the many difficulties he was to struggle with in carrying on such stupendous work in a new-settled country, all marshes and wilderness, producing nothing to subsist the multitudes of men in continual employment; all supplies for that purpose being entirely derived from old Russia.

The Tsar proceeded to augment the navy with sundry galleys; and about 1708 set up two ships of 52 guns each, at Lodeinoé Polé on the Ladoga Lake, under the care of Mr. Bent; one he finished,

required for higher ones' (*Biografiskt Lexikon öfver Namnkunnige Svenske Män*, vol. viii.; Stockholm, 1876; p. 364).

[1] MS. 'Harwaldy.' 'Between Karavalda island and Stirs point at 12 miles N. by W. of it lies the entrance to St. Petersburg Bay' (*Baltic Pilot*, ii. p. 292).

but, dying about 1710, left the other imperfect. Two more of equal force were also assigned to Mr. Brown.

The famous victory of Poltava on the 27th of June, 1709, creating in the Tsar too great an opinion of his military puissance, occasioned him in his war with the Turk to commit the error so fatal to the late King of Sweden, in marching his army too far into his enemy's country without securing a retreat in case of necessity. The event of this inconsideration was the loss sustained after the battle of Pruth,[1] in the subsequent capitulation; wherewith the Tsar, being obliged to deliver up Asof and Taganrog, rendered all his naval armament on the river Don entirely useless. Some of the ships were sent to Constantinople, either sold or given to the Turks; many burned by the Tsar's order, and others still remain at Taveroff under sheds to preserve them from the weather.[2] The equipment provided, espe-

[1] The allusion is to Peter's well-known campaign of 1711 on the Pruth. The desperate condition to which he was then reduced is shown by the letter which he sent to the Senate: 'I inform you that I with all my army, through no fault or mistake, but through false information, being surrounded by forces four times as strong, and cut off from all lines of supply, look forward—unless with special help of God—to nothing but complete destruction or captivity amongst the Turks. In the latter case you are no longer to look upon me as your Tsar and ruler, and are to do nothing which I tell you, even if I write it with my own hand, until I reappear amongst you in my own person. Should I perish, and authentic news of my death reach you, choose amongst yourselves the one most worthy to be my successor.' The Tsar and his army were extricated from the position thus indicated by the treaty made at Hush. In accordance with its terms Peter surrendered Asof and all his recent conquests in the region near; and undertook to level the lately constructed fortifications of Taganrog, Kammenoi Saton, and Bogorodizk (Herrmann, *Gesch. russ. Staates*, iv. pp. 270-1). His project of a Black Sea fleet was destroyed.

[2] 'Quant à la flotille du Don, bloquée à Voronéje par l'absence de fonds d'eau suffisants, elle ne pourra être utilisée en 1711 à la

cially sails and cordage, has since been carried sledge-ways to Archangel, when the Tsar built ships there in 1714. Two obstructions he then laboured under, and would again should he once more be master of Asof and Taganrog; one, his ships must be built up at Taveroff, near Voronezh, a great distance from Asof; and the river Don being very rapid it is difficult transporting them down : the other, at the mouth of this river for 9 or 10 leagues [there] being shoal water, he must build his men-of-war much flatter than usual, and yet after all apply wooden floats to lift and support them, till they reach the deep water : so that the Turks, by planting a few ships in station there, may easily prevent the Tsar from bringing his fleet to sea.

IV. EARLY SERVICES OF THE NEW BALTIC FLEET.

The first service ever done the Tsar by his ships built at St. Petersburg was in the entrance of the year 1710, when provisions, ammunition, and artillery were sent to carry on the siege of Viborg. A snow, commanded by Lieutenant Smith and sent into the Swedes' fleet with a flag of truce for exchange of some particular prisoners, being detained by the Swedes, as construing it a design to observe their strength; the Tsar by way of reprisal, when the town surrendered on the 13th of June following, made the garrison prisoners of war contrary to the capitulation. Hitherto the Tsar having served as Captain-Commodore,[1] now assumed the character of Rear-Admiral.

reprise des hostilités avec la Turquie. Après la perte d'Azof elle deviendra inutilisable. On en cédera une partie aux Turcs eux-mêmes, et on laissera pourrir le reste' (Waliszewski, *Pierre le Grand*, p. 556).

[1] The derivation of 'Commodore' is uncertain. We probably, like the Swedes, adopted it from the Dutch, who spelt the word

The Swedes hindering the victualling of the Russian garrison in Viborg this summer necessitated an early supply in the spring. The ice in the river Neva, by St. Petersburg, usually breaks up between the 5th and 15th of April; in 8 or 10 days more descends the ice from the Ladoga Lake; and by the latter end of the month the river is perfectly free: but then the Gulf of Finland is seldom clear for ships' passage till the 10th of May; and I have known ships stopped at Hogland, in the narrowest part of the Gulf, on the 13th of May. All requisite provision was made during the winter to proceed with the first open

Kommandeur. Apparently it was not known in our Navy till the early part of William III.'s time, when it was spelled both Commandore and Commadore. In Swedish the spelling is *Kommendör*, and in 1702 a Kommendör Karl Gustaf Löschern (von Hertsfeld) is mentioned. In a list of 1735 given by Bäckström (*Svenska Flottans Historia*, Stockholm, 1884, p. 426) the rank is so designated; but more recently, and at present, the official Swedish designation is *Kommendör-Kapten*. It has never been a permanent (or substantive) rank in the English service. In 1750 it was defined (E. Chambers' *Cyclopædia*) as the title of 'an Under-Admiral or officer commissioned by an Admiral to command a squadron of ships in chief.' The suggestion is that the designation was not recognised by the Admiralty. There is reason to believe that neither 'Commodore' nor 'Commander' as a present titular designation has anything to do directly with the verb 'command;' but that both are derived from 'commend' after these two verbs, notwithstanding their original identity, had been so fully differentiated from one another as to have acquired distinct meanings. In the old designation of the naval grade, just below that of post-captain, viz. 'Master *and* Commander,' the last word did imply command, the officer so designated being both the navigator and the captain of the ship. 'Commander' as now used—and 'Commodore' as a form of it—seem to be derived from 'commend' through *commendatio, in commendam*, &c., in connection with the holding of benefices. 'Commanderies' of the militant religious orders were essentially benefices, and not definite areas of military command. It is to these, and not to any exercise of military authority, that the dignity of Knights *Commanders* of the Bath, St. Michael and St. George, &c., refers. (See *New English Dictionary*.)

water; the Viborg and Riga, two men-of-war of 52 guns each, built by Mr. Brown, and launched in autumn, were ordered to strengthen the convoy. Two others of equal force were finished on the Ladoga Lake; one of them, commanded by Lieutenant Ivan Sinavin, was cast away coming down to the Fall; and the other, named the Pernau, arrived at St. Petersburg; but not time enough to join the fleet in this expedition. They sailed the beginning of May 1711, the variation in the breaking away of the ice above recounted favouring the Tsar by detaining the Swedish fleet from coming up the Gulf to oppose the passage of the Russian store-ships convoyed by the following men-of-war to Viborg:—

Flag Officers	Ships	Guns	Commanders
Vice-Admiral Cruys, Captain-Commodore Scheltinga	Viborg	52	De Cour
	Riga	52	—
—	Dumcraft	32	Besemacher
—	Standard	24	Wessel
—	Hobet	16	Waldron
—	Lesela (*snow*)	14	Ivan Sinavin
—	Moncure	14	Squerscoff

Highly pleased with their success, they soon returned to Kronslot.

About this time arrived the Samson, a frigate bought in Holland, and presented to the Tsar by Prince Menshikoff, whether as a mulct or a voluntary act was diversely conjectured. She mounted 40 guns, but, being too small for that number, was taken down to the lower water by Mr. Brown, and made an excellent frigate of 32 guns in the latter end of the year 1712. Now came the first oak timber the Tsar ever had, after almost three years spent in its transportation from Kazan; and forthwith several ships were clapped upon the stocks at St. Petersburg; and at Archangel a Hollander built of fir timber 3 ships of 52 guns each, and 3 frigates. The latter sailing from thence, one foundered; the other two, called the St. Peter and St. Paul, commanded by the Captains Rays and Brants, cruised in the North Sea: and taking several prizes from the Swedes, some from under the convoy of English men-of-war, wintered this year in Norway.[1]

V. OPERATIONS IN 1712.

In the spring 1712 the ships of war conducted a second supply of provisions to Viborg. The Pernau was brought down over the Bar and fitted for sea. In July the whole fleet lay ready to sail, when a Swedish man-of-war, a frigate, and a snow appeared in the offing. The Russ warped out in the night; and Vice-Admiral Cruys on board the Viborg striking his flag wore only a distinguishing pennant,[2] ordering the flag to be hoisted aboard the Dumcraft, that came not out of the haven. Early in the morning the Pernau, Samson and Lesela were ordered to give chase, attended by seven half-galleys [3] and as many brigantines to tow in case of a calm. The Swedes lay by expecting them; the Vice-Admiral observing it detached the Riga to their assistance; then the Swedes made off; and when the Russ were now within a league of the enemy, the Vice-Admiral

[1] Then part of the Danish kingdom.
[2] MS. 'pennon.' As an official term 'broad pennant' is correct. Nelson in a letter to the Admiral says 'broad pennant' (February 12, 1785), but in writing to the Admiralty uses the term 'distinguishing pennant' (February 17, 1785).—Laughton, *Nelson's Letters and Desp.*, pp. 29, 30, 31. See *post*, p. 121, where the author uses the word 'broad.'
[3] Half-galley, 'a sort of smaller galley with lighter armament' (*Studier öfver Svenska Skärgårds-Flottans Historia*, &c.—anonymous, but apparently by Mankell—Stockholm, 1855, p. 25).

made a signal to leave off chasing. The Swedes bore down upon them and, the Vice-Admiral giving the signal to renew the chase, the Swedes again endeavoured to make off. When they were just within gun shot the Vice-Admiral made the signal to come to an anchor; some random shot exchanged, the Russians returning anchored by their flag; and the Swedes under the north shore. The wind shifting by the next morning gave the Russ a great advantage, so that in two hours' space they might have cut off the Swedes' retreat; but, neglecting this opportunity, the Swedes plyed [1] to the windward and made the best of their way to sea. No more of them were seen this summer, except a small snow, taken by the Russ galleys near Wickolax when they plundered that place this year. In the winter Count de Buss, an Italian, Rear-Admiral of the galleys, exhibited a complaint of maleconduct against Vice-Admiral Cruys in the affair above related; but was not seaman enough to allege the most material faults committed. The right points of this charge were answered without much immediate prejudice to Vice-Admiral Cruys' character.

A LIST OF THE FLEET, 1712.

Flag Officers	Ships	Guns	Commanders
Vice-Admiral Cruys	Viborg	52	De Gruijter
—	Riga	52	Besemacher
—	Pernau	52	Edwards
—	Samson	40	Blorey
—	Standard	24	Wessel
—	Hobet	16	Waldron
—	Lesela	14	Sinavin
—	Moncure	14	Squerscoff

About this time Hadley and Johnston, two

[1] See note 5, p. 32, *post*.

builders assistants, were sent in quality of purveyors to prepare and mould the timber at Kazan. The two frigates St. Peter and St. Paul wintered at Riga, and the St. Jacob, a small frigate bought in Holland, at Revel. Two shipbuilders and several sea-officers arrived from Voronezh; and several brigantines, such as our sloops in England, were built at Ijora,[1] on a small river running into the Neva six leagues above St. Petersburg. The Katharina of 60 guns, built by Mr. Brown, a complete ship of war, was finished and launched in the spring; as also the Poltava, a 54-gun ship, the Tsar [being] principal builder. She was much too lean abaft and could never endure to ride in a great sea. Preparations were made this winter to invade Finland in the spring by sea and land. The Tsar chiefly wanting seamen ordered all away from the other side of his dominions, and broke several regiments of soldiers that had seen something at sea, to enroll them amongst his sailors and make up his complement.

VI. OPERATIONS IN 1713.

The General-Admiral, commanding in chief, sent away part of the army, and sailed the beginning of May 1713 with a fleet of near 200 galliots, *chalks*, smacks, galleys and brigantines, with two bomb galliots and as many *prahms*[2] of 16 large cannon

[1] MS. 'Esore;' Ijora or Izhora.

[2] Prahm—Dutch, *praam* : 'In general a vessel with a quite flat bottom used to load ships, transport artillery and men across rivers; because, not being deep in the water, she can come nearer the shore. At the present day [prahms] are fitted out as large ships of war. Though the bottom retains its form, they are fitted with three masts and the sails appertaining to them. In 1715 in the expedition to Rügen and Stralsund against the Swedes, the King of Denmark made use of ships of war of this kind : and in

each, passing within the rocks and islands directly to Helsingfors. The Admiral was on board a galley, and the Tsar in another, having quitted the snow Moncure because she could not keep up with the headmost. Some galleys directed to row ahead to inspect the state of the place, coming near and observing a Lübeck ship hauled up close under a small battery of 4 guns, brought her off with the loss of several men, killed and wounded. Being newly arrived and her lading principally wines, she proved a good prize to the superior officers. The whole fleet coming up the next day, the two *prahms* were ordered to cannonade the batteries, whilst the bomb galliots played [on], and set the town on fire. The Swedes, driven from their batteries, contributed to increase the flames, and made their retreat in the evening. The Russ troops landed in the night, and the Tsar early in the morning; bestowing the plunder on his Preobrojensky, or Life, Guards and strictly prohibiting all others to touch the spoil. The Swedes, as reported, in number 6,000 were commanded by General Armfelt,[1] and had two batteries consisting of 6 guns, 6-pounders only.

1717 and 1718 the Imperialists used them on the Danube with good effect against the Turks. The name "prahm," or "decked prahm," is also given to low vessels with ordinary block-houses built on them, in which loop-holes for infantry as well as port-holes for a couple of guns are cut' (Zedler's *Lexikon*, vol. xxix.; 1741; p. 182).

[1] Carl Gustaf Armfelt, born November 9, 1666. In 1685 went to France, served in the French armies for seventeen months as a volunteer, and remained altogether in France for twelve years. Was present at several actions and at the sieges at Nice, Villa Franca, Susa, Valenciennes, and Ath. In 1701 Adjutant-General of the army in Finland; Major-General, 1711; Lieutenant-General, 1717; Baron, 1731; General and Commander-in-Chief of the troops in Finland, 1735. Died October 24, 1736. Had nineteen children (*Biografiskt Lexikon öfver Namnkunnige Svenske Män*, vol. i.; Stockholm, 1874; p. 243).

After the ruin of this place the Fleet sailed back to Borgö; and the inhabitants deserting their habitations on the approach of the Russ, the army landed and joined the part that had marched upon Viborg, proceeding in their conquests this summer as far as Åbö. Soon after 5 large Holland flyboats, arriving at Helsingfors to load timber, were all burned, and the men either killed or wounded in a barbarous manner by Count de Buss, Rear-Admiral of the Russian galleys, merely through ignorance and indistinction of the neutral flags and passes. This action was utterly unjustifiable, Admiral Apraxin gave him a severe reprimand and sent the report to the Tsar, at that time returned to St. Petersburg to hasten his fleet of men-of-war to sea. Most of the English and Dutch officers in the late expedition were remanded back to man their ships; and Captain Sievers, with several officers, ordered to Revel to take care of several ships arrived from abroad.

A List of the Fleet of Men-of-War, 1713.

Flag Officers	Ships	Guns	Commanders
Vice-Admiral Cruys	Riga	52	Degruijter
Captain-Commodore Scheltinga . .	Viborg	52	Blorey
Captain-Commodore Rays . . .	Poltava	54	Turnhoud
—	Katharina	60	Gosler
—	Pernau	52	Besemacher
—	Samson	32	Edwards
—	St. Paul	30	Wessel
—	St. Peter	30	Brant
—	Standard	24	Papagoy
—	St. Jacob	16	Falkenberg
—	Lesela	14	Trane

All the captains are to be removed, and

frequently are so twice or thrice in a summer, for reasons of moment hereafter specified in due place. The lists here presented regard them at the commencement of the campaign without tracing them through their reiterated changes. Also in the Tsar's service are Captain-lieutenants, often commanding ships of the line as well as frigates, and are equal to captains in all points aboard their respective ships. Only they are allowed two men less for a guard on board a flag ship, and receive 5 roubles [1] per month less pay than the youngest rank captains. This premised, no distinction will be used for the future in the title, when the captain-lieutenants command in chief.

This fleet sailed from Kronslot the beginning of July 1713 for Revel; where the Tsar expected the arrival of sundry ships bought for his use in England and Holland. In their passage down the Gulf of Finland [2] some frigates were ordered to sail a good distance ahead of the fleet, and report by signals to the flag if they saw any strange ships. Near Hogland they spied three sail, proving to be Swedes' men-of-war from 64 to 54 guns; [3] and upon

---

[1] As to relative value of the rouble, see *post*, p. 99, *note* 2.
[2] MS. 'Finns' Gulph.'
[3] The Swedish account of this is as follows· 'In July, 1713, a squadron under Vice-Admiral Erik Johan Lillie's command went to Helsingfors, and from that squadron three ships—one of 56, one of 54, and one of 48 guns—were sent for a cruise under Commodore Karl Raab's command. After this division had taken several prizes, and had reconnoitred the enemy's position at Revel, it anchored off Hogland on July 10. On the next morning at sunrise the Russian fleet, of 14 ships of the line and frigates, was seen coming from the eastward with a fair wind; and, as Raab could not involve himself in a fight with an enemy so superior, he kept off and ordered his ships to support each other as well as they could. The Russian had begun to chase the Swedes at ½ past 2 in the morning; but the latter replied so heavily to the Russian fire that two Russian ships were soon dis-

making the proper signal the whole Russ fleet gave chase. Some of the headmost came up and fired, but at too great a distance, the Russ powder being much inferior to the Swedish. In this chase the Riga, with Vice-Admiral Cruys on board, struck upon a rock; and immediately after the Viborg with Captain-Commodore Scheltinga. The rest continued the chase; but Captain-Commodore Rays not taking the command upon him, nor giving any signal, they all returned in a little time to the flag, and got the Riga off without much damage; but the wind blowing pretty fresh in the evening the Viborg bilged,[1] and they set her on fire. The Swedes in this encounter,[2] by keeping in a regular line and seconding each other, awed the Russians; and at parting made several shots after them by way of defiance. The Russ fleet proceeding to Revel were there joined by five ships arrived from England, the Victory, Lansdowne, Oxford, Randolph, and Strafford; as also by two ships, the St. Antonio and St.

masted. A third had to lie to to stop a bad leak: but the Viborg, the Russian Vice-Admiral's ship, came close up to the Swedish ships, and somewhat later the Russian Admiral's ship, Moskva, also the remaining Russian ships were worse sailers and were much farther astern. The chase was continued till 8 o'clock, when the Swedish senior officer's ship, Ösel, ran on a shoal; but Raab set all sail and succeeded in getting over the bank: the Moskva, however [we see from the text that it was the Viborg], stuck so fast that she could not be got off, so that, after the crew had been saved, the Russians themselves set fire to their flag-ship. The Viborg also grounded, but less heavily. In the meantime Raab with his ships succeeded in getting to Helsingfors' (Bäckström, *Svenska Flottans-Historia*, p. 178). This was the first occasion on which the Russian fleet really engaged an enemy at sea.

[1] The MS. has 'bulged,' for which the word 'bilged,' as being more generally used, has been substituted. Both words are right. 'Bulged, . . . †2. Of a ship with the bottom or sides stove in.' 'Bilge.— 1. *trans.*, to stave in a ship's bottom, &c.' (*New English Dictionary*).

[2] MS. 'recounter.'

Nicholas, from Hamburg. The Bolingbroke, another English ship of 52 guns, being taken in its passage by the Swedes. After some stay they returned to Kronslot, and thus ended this summer's expedition of the ships of war. But the galleys under the Lord High Admiral continued much longer out, the Tsar going to Helsingfors a second time this year, to push on the building of a fortress on the plan of the demolished town; essaying at the same time to bar up the several passages into the harbour, one only excepted with a very narrow entrance lined on each side with batteries of heavy cannon. Two brigantines commanded by foreign officers were sent to make a chart from Helsingfors to Hogland. The two *prahms* with several galleys wintered in this port, the rest returning to St. Petersburg. The new haven at Revel was begun this winter, and considerably advanced under the directions of Major Lubrass, an engineer.

VII. COURTS-MARTIAL.

The ships laid up and the rivers frozen, about the latter end of November a court-martial was called to examine into the conduct of Vice-Admiral Cruys and Captains-Commodores Scheltinga and Rays. Cruys was tried on the precedent information of Count de Buss the foregoing year, as also with Scheltinga and Rays for misbehaviour in the affair with the three Swedish ships this year.

THE MEMBERS OF THE COURT-MARTIAL.

Lord High Admiral Count Apraxin (*President*).
Rear-Admiral Peter Alexeievitz (*The Tsar*).
Captain-Commodore Alexander Menshikoff.

Captains.	{ Peter Sievers. Cronenburg.[1] Nelson.
Captain-Lieutenant.	Bering.[2]
Lieutenants.	{ Conon Zotoff. Zacharia Mishecoft.

Notwithstanding this court usually met by 4 o'clock in the morning, and never missed a day unless upon extraordinary occasions, yet they were near three months before they came to a determinate resolution. At last in February notice was given to all officers, that had a mind to hear the sentence pronounced, to appear. The room was not half large enough to receive the audience; however, the President began with the sentence of Vice-Admiral Cruys as follows :

For not having embraced the opportunity of taking or destroying the two Swedish ships and one snow in 1712, and when, in chase of three Swedish ships of war in 1713, his own ship struck on a rock, for not going on board another ship to hoist his flag and pursue the enemy; not giving the signal to the other commanding officers to board or pursue; for neglect of duty in these articles he was by the court adjudged to lose his life, but his Majesty had mitigated the sentence, and he must next day be sent into banishment to Kazan. To this he replied with a bow, 'What his Majesty pleases.' This sentence was again read over to him in Hollands[3] by Captain Sievers, and he answered as before.

Then the court sentenced Captain-Commodore Scheltinga for not taking the command upon him, to

---

[1] MS. 'Crownbergh.'
[2] Vitus Jonassen Bering, the famous discoverer. Born 1681 at Horsens, in Denmark; died December 19, 1741.
[3] Dutch.

serve as youngest captain during his Majesty's pleasure.

Last of all Captain-Commodore Rays' sentence was published; importing that seeing his two commanding officers were, by their ships striking on the rocks, rendered incapable of pursuing the enemy; and he had not taken the command upon him, nor made use of the excellent opportunity to take or destroy the enemy's three ships: for this act of cowardice he was condemned by the court to be carried to the place of execution, and immediately to be shot to death. In pursuance of the sentence he was directly led to the post, but a few paces distant; and a file of musketeers being ready, the word of command was given to present their arms, when the Tsar's pardon was read, implying the change of his punishment into a perpetual banishment in Siberia. The fear of death had seized him with that violence that when they lifted up his cap from over his eyes, and took him up from his knees, he said in the Russian tongue, 'Luchey Polley' (*'Tis better shoot me*). He was carried to an adjacent house, and let blood, and in two or three days' time sent into exile, where lingering a few years he died in Siberia, being never perfectly recovered from the effects of his fright. The proceedings of this court-martial are the more minutely particularised, as being in some circumstances, I believe, unprecedented till that time, and in consequence made some noise in the world.

Several galleys were built this winter; and many officers advanced, Scheltinga restored, and Sievers raised to the rank of Commodore. Captain Andrew Simpson, sent from Asof with 4 ships to Constantinople after the capitulation of Pruth, was upon his return commanded to bring round to the Baltic the three ships built at Archangel in 1711 with the assistance of Captains Cramer and Webhamey. These were now expected; but, being obliged to impress men out of the foreign merchants' service to carry their ships to sea, meeting also with bad weather, and the season of the year too far expired, Cramer put back and wintered at Archangel: Webhamey got into the river of Kola and wintered in Lapland, where he was discharged and Captain Ivan Sinavin sent to succeed him; and Simpson, reaching Norway, wintered near Trondhjem.

VIII. PROCEEDINGS IN 1714.

The Russians made extraordinary preparations in fitting out their fleet this spring (1714). Several of the Tsar's officers having learned in Germany the art of gunnery, &c., upon their return got a company allowed under the title of Bombardiers. These are well paid, and distributed as occasion requires on board the ships. Some new inventions were devised of the combustible kind for destroying of ships, and reeds ready filled with prepared powder for the quicker firing of guns; two vessels furnished with fire-spouts, or engines spouting liquid fire; and just before the fleet sailed, the Tsar ordered boarding [1] bridges to be fixed with hinges to the gunwale [2] of every ship, from the entering place to the forecastle reclining upon the booms; but in time of action, in case of boarding [1] easily revolving upon the enemy's gunwale to facilitate the entrance of his men.

[1] In this sentence 'boarding' is used, in one case, in a sense quite different from that in which it is used in the other. In the first it means putting a party of men on board the enemy's ship with the object of capturing her sword in hand. The old word for this was 'entering' (comp. Swedish *äntring*). In the second case it means 'falling on board of,' 'fouling' the other ship.
[2] MS. 'gunnel.'

UNDER PETER THE GREAT

The General-Admiral departed with the galleys to prosecute his conquests on the side of Finland, where he commanded in chief by sea and land. A general expectation prevailed of something extraordinary to be done this summer, on account of the penalties inflicted on the omissions of the two foregoing years, the considerable increase of the fleet, when reinforced by the ships appointed to join at Revel ; and the Tsar's resolution to command himself in person.

A LIST OF THE FLEET, 1714.

Flag Officers	Ships	Guns	Commanders
Rear-Admiral Peter Alexeievitz . .	Katharina	60	Gosler
Captain-Commodore Scheltinga . .	Poltava	54	Griese
Captain-Commodore Sievers . .	Victory	60	Turnhoud
—	Riga	52	Cronenburg
—	Pernau	52	Besemacher
—	Randolph	50	Wessel
—	Oxford	50	Van Gent
—	St. Anthony	50	Van Hofft
—	Strafford	50	Nelson
—	Lansdowne	40	Huyck
—	Samson	32	Brant
—	St. Paul	30	Bredale
—	St. Peter	30	Eckoff
—	St. Jacob	16	Falkenberg
—	Princess (*snow*)	16	Muconoff
—	Natalia ,,	14	Blorey
—	Diana ,,	14	Trane

This fleet sailing from Kronslot on the 20th of May to Biörkö Sound, some frigates cruised to Hogland till the latter end of the month ; when the whole fleet proceeding thither arrived at Revel by the 11th of June ; and were there joined by the St.

Michael and Raphael from Arkhangel, the[1] Le Firme, Ormonde, Fortune and Arundel from England, and L'Espérance from Holland. Some of these ships met with great difficulties in their passage. The St. Michael, Captain Simpson, first amused and then ran by a Swedish squadron in spite of their force; and Captain Purnel, a gentleman that brought over several ships to the Tsar, escaped in the Le Firme by pure outsailing. Also at this port were arrived from England the Captains Vaughan, Rue, Baker and Fitch, with several lieutenants and surgeons, under the Government's permission; and some of the last two characters from Holland. Vaughan was sent to fetch the Pearl, a ship bought in Holland, and chased into Pernau by the Swedes. Several of the ships were hauled into the haven to exchange and size [2] their guns. The new captains were appointed their respective commands, and the men divided into their proper complements; the snow Diana despatched with a flag of truce and letters from the Tsar to find out the enemy: the Samson, Captain Brant, ordered to cruise on the east; and the St. Paul, Captain Bredale, on the west sides of the island Nargen; in hourly expectation of the Swedes.

On the 19th at 4 in the afternoon Captain Bredale in the St. Paul discovered six sail of large ships coming right afore a westerly wind for Revel; upon a nearer approach they perceived them to be ships of war, all with English colours, and a snow in company. The captain sent his lieutenant in the pinnace to acquaint the Rear-Admiral; but, not finding him aboard, went directly ashore and made his report to the Tsar at his country house about

---

[1] The author generally speaks of this ship as though 'Le' were part of the name and not the article.

[2] Arrange their ordnance so as to carry the guns assigned to ships of each rate.

half a mile from the town. The Tsar, so I style him ashore, though he would be addressed by no other name than that of Rear-Admiral on board, immediately ordered the signal of alarm to be given and all the ships in harbour to haul out forthwith ; sending back the lieutenant with directions to his captain and the captain of the Samson to keep dodging of the enemy, but not go nearer than the reach of a random [1] shot, adding that he with the whole fleet would be out in the morning by daylight. The whole night was spent by the Russ in getting their ships out of the haven, and other preparations for the ensuing day. The Swedes standing off and on all night between the Island Nargen and Stirs point,[2] early in the morning, being 6 men-of-war from 64 to 54 guns under the command of Vice-Admiral Lillie,[3] hoisted their proper colours, and making sail came fairly into Revel Bay at the instant the Russian fleet were all under sail coming out. After the Swedes were got far enough in to count their numbers and observe their motions, the Vice-Admiral made the signal to tack : the St. Paul being pretty near, the hindmost of the Swedes fired at her to try, as supposed, the difference

---

[1] 'Random shot—a shot made when the muzzle of the gun is raised above the horizontal line and is not designed to shoot directly or point-blank. The utmost *random* of any piece is about ten times as far as the bullet will go point-blank ; and the bullet will go farthest when the piece is mounted [*sic*; 'elevated' is meant] about 45 degrees above the level range. The space or distance of the *random* is reckoned from the platform to the place where the bullet first grazes' (E. Chambers, F.R.S., *Cyclopædia*, 1750, vol. ii.). A 'random shot' had, therefore, a well-understood range, and was not a shot fired anyhow or 'at random.' The range for a medium ship's gun was perhaps from 1,000 to 1,200 yards, according to the piece fired.

[2] MS. 'the Point of Surps.' Stirs Point is at the entrance to St. Petersburg Bay (*Baltic Pilot*, ii. p. 292).

[3] Erik Johan Lillie.

of their powder [1]; the shot just reached, but the St. Paul returning the fire the ball fell at least one-third short of the enemy. About 7 in the morning the Swedish Admiral gave the signal for the line of battle, and having formed kept plying out.[2] Captain-Commodore Scheltinga made the same signal on the Russ side, the Tsar having struck his flag two days before. Also the Arundel ran upon the Middle Ground, a shoal betwixt Nargen and Karl[3] island; half an hour after, the Swedes dismissed the snow Diana, and she joined the Russ fleet; at 11 the Arundel got off; and by noon some of the Russian ships were within a league of the Swedes, all still continuing the chase. The wind this forenoon was from West to West South West a moderate gale, but at 1 o'clock[4] veered to north west; at the same time a signal was made from the snow Princess, and repeated by Captain-Commodore Scheltinga, for the fleet to make more sail. This snow kept about a league's distance from the headmost of the Russ, and the officers discovered by this signal that the Tsar had quitted his ship: whereas all expected he would have kept aboard without hoisting his flag: however, the chase continued and several galleys and brigantines came up from Revel to tow the ships in case of a calm. There was not much wind this afternoon and the Swedes, apprehensive of the disadvantage if a calm should ensue, made their utmost efforts to get out to sea; but one of them, not sailing so well as the rest, in turning out [5] was about an English mile to the leeward.[6] At 5 in the evening,

[1] MS. 'power;' but 'powder' seems to be meant. (See p. 24.)
[2] Beating, or working out.
[3] MS. 'the Carles.'   [4] MS. 'one a clock.'
[5] Working or beating out. 'Turning out' was in use amongst Elizabethan seamen. (See *N.R.S.*, i. p. 288.)
[6] In modern times we have dropped 'the' before 'windward' and 'leeward.'

about seven Russ ships and two frigates came so near that, at the next tack, or in three-quarters of an hour's space, they must engage this hindermost ship. At this juncture the Vice-Admiral hauled up his lower sails and bore down before the wind, still keeping in line of battle, to the ship in danger ; and receiving her into her station kept upon a wind under his topsails. This resolute behaviour of the brave Swede, determined to lose all or none, daunted the Russ, so that, willing to have the rest of the fleet—some one, others two leagues astern—come up to their assistance, they stood longer than usual upon the next tack: for they might upon going about have fetched the enemy. But they knew not how to act ; some that had shown great forwardness, upon the prospect of half a dozen engaging a single ship, now acted the quite reverse ; not trimming their sails, making bad steerage, &c. The Katharina, one of the best sailers and the best manned, wherein the Tsar sailed whilst in the fleet, and by far the best of the headmost ships, had her mizen[1] topsail aback near an hour. In this uncertainty they observed a signal from the snow Princess to bear away for Revel, she having borne away to make the fleet the better observe her. This was but little expected ; however, all knew it was from the Tsar. Some immediately conformed and the rest followed the example of Commodore Scheltinga upon his repetition of the signal. The Swedish Vice-Admiral fired two shot at the Russ galleys. It was still little wind, and very uncertain. Had there been a gale to be depended upon, 'tis thought the Swedes would have attacked the Russians in their return.[2]

[1] MS. 'missen.'
[2] The Swedish naval historian, Bäckström, makes no mention of this.

An exact list of the ships and commanders in this chase :—

Flag Officers	Ships	Guns	Commanders
—	Katharina	64	Gosler
Captain-Commodore Scheltinga	Poltava	54	Griese
—	Riga	52	Cronenburg
—	Pernau	52	Besemacher
—	St. Antonio	50	Van Hofft
—	St. Michael	52	Simpson
—	St. Raphael	52	Ivan Sinevin
Captain-Commodore Sievers	Le Firme	70	Turnhoud
—	Randolph	50	Wessel
—	Ormonde	50	Rue
—	L'Espérance	46	Edwards
—	Arundel	46	Fitch
—	Lansdowne	40	Huyck
—	Samson	32	Brant
—	St. Paul	30	Bredale
—	St. Peter	30	Eckoff
—	Princess (*snow*)	16	Muconoff
—	Natalia ,,	14	Blorey
—	Diana ,,	14	Trane
—	Seven Galleys		
—	Nine Brigantines		

Left in the harbour for want of officers and men, the Victory, Oxford, Strafford, and Fortune. It is true some of the ships in the list above could not have come up to engage in several hours; being as yet detained in getting their men and ammunition on board: and some others had not time to quarter their men, and adjust several things pre-requisite to an engagement.

IX. *THE AFFAIR OF HANGO HEAD—DEFEAT OF THE SWEDES*, 1714.

The Russ fleet lay in Revel Bay, daily exercising their men, and some ships constantly out a-cruising 4 or 5 leagues off; when about the 30th of this month arrived a brigantine express from Helsingfors with advice that the General-Admiral with his galleys was pent up near Hangö Head by 16 sail of Swedes men-of-war, besides several frigates, a *prahm*, and 6 galleys. Upon the arrival of this news the Tsar ordered Captain Bredale of the St. Paul to hold his ship in readiness, determining to go over in person the first fair wind to view the posture of the Swedes, and advise with his Admiral. After two or three unsuccessful attempts, the wind not proving favourable, he at last reached Helsingfors by the 19th of July, and proceeded thence in a galley to Hangö Head attended by Captain-Commodore Sievers and Captain Bredale. They found the Swedish fleet lying at anchor off the point of an isthmus, or neck of land, extended at proper distance a great way into the sea, in order to intercept the Russ galleys whenever they should move from within the little islands and rocks, where they now lay secure from insults; waiting for a calm that frequently intervenes at this season of the year, wherein they might in a few hours' space by the use of their oars get clear. In the mean time to amuse the Swedes, the Russ made a show of hauling their galleys over the neck of land; and this point succeeded so well that Rear-Admiral Ehrenskiöld[1] was ordered to remove with the 6 galleys, 2 shear-boats,[2] and the *prahm* mounted with 14 cannon, and

[1] MS. 'Earnshild.' Even the Swedes are not agreed upon the spelling of this heroic Admiral's name. Bäckström spells it Ehrensköld. In the Swedish biographical dictionary—the spelling of which is here followed—the name is Ehrenskiöld. Nils Ehrenskiöld, born at Åbo, May 11, 1674; died at Karlskrona, November 2, 1728. Entered the naval service in 1692. Captain of the Liffland, 1700. After the action he was kept a prisoner-of-war till the peace of Nystadt, 1721.

[2] These are the 'skärbåtar' (pronounced *shareboat*) of the Swedes.

post himself so as to prevent the launching of the Russ galleys on the other side of the isthmus. They also dispatched about 7 men-of-war to find out a passage in amongst the rocks and islands on the farthermost side of the Russ galleys, that, by inclosing them within the two squadrons, they might, if possible, destroy them. The Russ observed all their designs, and the long looked for calm at length fortunately offering, the galleys began to move under the command of Commodore Ismaiwitz. Captain Bredale led the way, and the rest followed; some close by the shore, and others betwixt the Swedes men-of-war, whilst they in vain endeavoured to hinder their passing by random shot, doing little execution on account of the smallness of their[1] bulk and swiftness of their motion. Only one galley striking on a rock was taken. After they had escaped the ships, the Tsar sent his favourite, the Adjutant-General Paul Jagosinski, with a white flag to summon Rear-Admiral Ehrenskiöld with the *prahm* and galleys under his command to surrender; signifying the impossibility of escaping, and reasonableness of preventing the effusion of Christian blood: promising civil usage to himself and people if, accepting this offer, he would forthwith strike his flag and submit to the Tsar; but in case of refusal he would assuredly meet with a furious attack and be taken by force, and then whoever survived the action must expect no better treatment than common prisoners-of-war. The Rear-Admiral replied, 'I have spent my life in the service of my King and country with inviolable fidelity, and as I have lived so I resolve to die in maintaining these interests. The Tsar has nothing to expect from me, or any under my command, but a vigorous defence; and if

---

[1] *I.e.* the boats'.

he resolves to have us, we will dispute it with him inch by inch to the last gasp.'

Upon the report of this answer to the Tsar he ordered about 35 galleys to be got clear, well manned and furnished with all things necessary; appointing particular officers to command. Nor was the Swedish Rear-Admiral idle, for, knowing he should be overpowered with numbers, he placed his galleys in an excellent posture of defence, so that the Russ could only board the two wings at a time; and due provision was made for their retreat from vessel to vessel whilst any remained untaken. After these preparations [1] the Russian galleys came down upon them and a bloody combat ensued; the Swedes asserting every step and, when no longer able to resist, retiring from galley to galley; last of all threw themselves into the *prahm*, wherein the Rear-Admiral abode during the whole engagement, and maintained it with the last obstinacy till most of the men were slain, the Rear-Admiral dangerously wounded, and the *prahm* herself [2] on fire. Then the Russ boarding [3] struck her flag, and extinguished the flames, whilst the Rear-Admiral in his boats, under the head of the *prahm*, attempting to get ashore, was taken by Captain Bredale. The Tsar beheld this action from an island at some distance; and

[1] Levesque (*Hist. de Russie*, iv. p. 421) and Mankell (*Studier öfver Svenska Skärgårds-Flottans Hist.* p. 21) give the date as July 27. Bäckström (*Svenska Flottans Historia*, p. 179) gives it as July 26. Waliszewski (*Pierre le Grand*, p. 557) says it was July 25. Whilst Herrmann (*Gesch. russ. Staates*, iv. p. 285) increases the confusion by saying that the fight took place on $\frac{July\ 26}{August\ 7}$.

[2] MS. 'itself,' which shows that the copyist was, probably, not a seaman.

[3] The word 'boarding' is here used in the modern sense of sending on board armed men to fight it out with the ship's crew on the deck. As stated in a former note the old word for this was 'entering.'

when over [1] came aboard, ordering particular care to be taken of the Rear-Admiral, though his wounds were reported mortal and he contracted by them an incurable lameness. He was carried to St. Petersburg, where he kept his bed several months in a lodging near the Palace, attended by that Prince's own physicians and surgeons; and enjoyed a handsome allowance till the late peace. Soon after this defeat the late King of Sweden [2] appointed him Vice-Admiral; and returning home since the conclusion of the war his present Majesty,[3] to whom the Tsar recommended him, constituted him Admiral. The loss on both sides was considerable; but as it is a maxim with them [4] to conceal the number of the slain, reports widely differing, I leave it undetermined. The St. Paul was sent with the news to the Tsarina at Revel, where great rejoicings were made, and couriers dispatched to notify the same through all Russia. The galleys proceeded to Åbö and overran a fresh part of Finland.

[1] This is a hitherto unreported fact about this galley action. It has always been stated by historians that Peter took an active part in the action, boarding the Swedish small craft in person. In the Swedish biographical dictionary (article Ehrenskiöld) it is said that 'The Tsar boarded the Swedish Admiral's vessel, Elefant, and took both her and the Commander' (*Czaren äntrade Svenska Amiral-skeppet, &c.*). The Swedes give Ehrenskiöld's force as 1 prahm, 6 galleys, and 2 boats (*skärbåtar*), with 900 men; and they put the Russian flotilla at 115 galleys and 20,000 men (Bäckström, pp. 179, 180; Mankell, pp. 21, 22). On the Swedish side they say that 700 were killed and wounded, and on the Russian 4,600. The affair—since known as the Battle of Hangö Head—was really a galley action which, though there was some firing, differed but little from those of ancient and mediæval times.

[2] Charles XII., died 1718.
[3] Frederick (Fredrik) I., died 1751.
[4] The Russians.

X. THE TSAR'S LANDING IN A GALE OF WIND —ARRANGEMENTS MADE AFTER THE END OF THE YEAR'S CAMPAIGN.

In July this year the Elias, a snow-frigate, arrived from St. Petersburg and with the Pearl from Pernau joined the fleet at Revel. In August, 12 of the principal ships, directed to winter at Kronslot, went over to Helsingfors and stayed there till the Tsar returned from Åbö, and then sailed to Biörkö Sound: but the Tsar, going before in a galley, met the fleet again off Biörkö Island and went on board his ship Katharina. In September, as they rode at anchor in the channel without the said island, it blew a hard gale of wind westerly; and, as usual after such a gale continued a while, the water driven up by the violence of the wind returning, with the addition of the water descending from the River Neva, occasioned a strong current running to windward, making what is called a hollow sea, exceeding troublesome for ships to ride in. Most of their boats astern of their ships were lost; and the Tsar, desirous of quitting that tumultuous element, asked his officers if any of them would venture to put him ashore. Lieutenant John Delap, a native of Ireland, undertook it. Upon a signal given a yawl was brought and, the Tsar getting in, Delap steered to Biörkö Island and set him safe ashore; receiving 100 roubles for his service, and out of which he was obliged to give the boat's crew thirty. One ship lost her foremast and bowsprit;[1] but, the wind in time abating, the fleet proceeded to Kronslot. The latter end of this month the Gabriel, Captain Cramer, from Archangel, having lost her mainmast, arrived at Revel: and the rest of the ships were

[1] MS. 'boltsprit.'

ordered to winter there, the haven being now esteemed a place of sufficient security.

This summer's expedition thus prosperously ended, the Rear-Admiral Peter Alexeievitz, on his arrival at St. Petersburg, was advanced to the rank of Vice-Admiral, having modestly refused this preferment before, whilst as yet he had not merited this dignity by any distinguishing action at sea. Several other officers were also promoted this winter, and medals struck in memory of the victory at Hangö Head distributed to the principal Commanders concerned therein. Rear-Admiral Tressel arrived from Holland, but dying before the next campaign this mention of him may suffice. Commissaries were established in the Navy with particular instructions, having also the charge of the victualling part heretofore managed by the officers of the soldiers on board each ship. Vice-Admiral Cruys was recalled, restored, and made Vice-President of the College of Admiralty[1]; but not to go to sea. This gentleman, a native of Norway, bred a sailor in Holland and advanced there, had in the last Dutch war been pretty active in privateering upon the English. Some little prejudices imbibed in his youth, through the ill understanding betwixt the two nations, did not easily wear off, and might probably render him less a friend to the English than otherwise he would have been. However, he is a man of sobriety, and a good seaman; and, notwithstanding some errors in judgment, has been of excellent service to the Tsar, indefatigably studying to improve the maritime affairs in opposition to the many difficulties industriously thrown in his way, out of envy to him as a foreigner, by the malevolent Russians.

[1] Or, as we should say, Board of Admiralty. *Kollegium* was the official term in Sweden for a Board, *e.g. Amiralitets-Kollegium.* (See note, *post*, p. 62).

Upon laying up the ships, the boarding bridges of such mighty expectation were quietly taken away, as it was impossible they should answer the design; so everybody with much caution forbore to speak of them, to avoid giving offence. In February were sent by sledgeway to Archangel, with several Lieutenants under officers and seamen, Ivan Sinavin, Vitus Bering, Peter Bents, and John Deane, appointed to command and bring round four ships of war a-building there by Peter Webby, son and successor to the builder mentioned in 1711. Captain-Commodore Scheltinga went into Holland to engage officers and seamen in his Tsarish Majesty's service, and forward three ships a-building there and expected to be ready in the spring. The Slutelburg and Narva, two 60-gun ships launched in autumn, were equipped, and the latter soon after blown up in the road at Kronslot, the powder taking fire by lightning: Captain-Commodore Vaughan and all the men were lost, except a lieutenant and three or four sailors. The St. Paul, Captain Bredale; the Samson, Captain Brant; the St. Peter, Captain Eckoff; and a snow were ordered out a-cruising upon intelligence received of some small Swedish privateers upon the coast of the Island Ösel: three whereof they took, and, burning one because leaky, brought in the other two, occasioning great rejoicings. Three ships bought in England arrived —the London, Britannia, and Richmond.

XI. *PROCEEDINGS IN* 1715.

Early this spring a Swedish squadron, consisting of 16 sail under the command of two flag officers, came into Revel Bay and cannonaded the ships in the haven at the distance of random shot; the Russ retaliating it from their batteries; but with inconsiderable damage on either side.

The ships of war sailed this year from Kronslot in June, and, arriving at Revel, joined the squadron that wintered there; forming, upon their union, the following fleet under the command of General-Admiral Apraxin :—

LIST OF THE FLEET, 1715.

Flag Officers	Ships	Guns	Commanders
General - Admiral Apraxin . .	Le Firme	70	Captain-Commodore Sievers
Vice-Admiral Peter Alexeievitz . .	Katharina	65	Gosler
Rear-Admiral Alexander Menshikoff	Slutelburg	64	Edwards
—	Poltava	54	Van Gent
—	St. Michael	52	Rue
—	Raphael	52	Ivan Sinavin
—	Gabriel	52	Cramer
—	Riga	52	Cronenburg
—	Pernau	52	Besemacher
—	Pearl	52	Griese
—	London	52	Huycke
—	Randolph	50	Wesel
—	Oxford	50	Blorey
—	St. Antonio	50	Van Hofft
—	Fortune	48	Baker
—	Richmond	46	Turnhoud
—	Arundel	46	Fitch
—	Samson	32	Brant
—	St. Paul	30	Bredale
—	St. Peter	30	Eckoff
—	Elias	28	Nelson
—	Princess (*snow*)	16	Muconoff
—	Lesela ,,	14	Batting

These ships were manned and cruised alternately at sea, the flags excepted: and besides these lay in the havens for want of men the Victory, Britannia, Ormonde, St. Nicholas, Strafford, and Lansdowne.

This fleet sailed in July from Revel, and put into Råger Wik;[1] where the Tsar, observing the situation of the place, had a plan drawn, the various depths of the water taken, and the width of the bay at the entrance measured with lines; determining the first favourable opportunity to build a haven there; if upon conclusion of the war he should keep possession of the Province. Seven sail of Russ ships out a-cruising, first discovered the British and Dutch squadron under the command of the Honourable Sir John Norris,[2] Admiral of the Blue; they passed in sight of Råger Wik on the 23rd of July, steering for Revel, where they had been before the beginning of June this year. The next day the Russian fleet returned to Revel and anchored in a half moon betwixt the British squadron and the shore. About a fortnight was spent in a mutual exchange of civilities betwixt them; and the 2nd of August Admiral Norris entertained the Tsar, Tsarina, and the Russian Court in a very splendid magnificent manner.

About this time, Count de Buss being dead, Captain-Commodore Ismaivitz was advanced to the rank of Rear-Admiral of the Galleys, succeeding

[1] MS. 'Rogerwyck.'
[2] Admiral of the Fleet Sir John Norris, born 1660, died 1749. Third son of Tho. Norris of Speke, Lancashire, and Katherine, daughter of Sir Henry Garraway. Lieut. of the Edgar, 1689. Commander of the Pelican, fire-ship, 1690. Posted January 13, 169$\frac{2}{3}$, in the Sheerness, frigate. Rear-Admiral, 1707; Vice-Admiral, 1708; Admiral 1709. Sat in the House of Commons several times for Portsmouth and for Rye. First Captain of the Britannia, flag-ship of the joint Commanders-in-Chief, Sir C. Shovell and Earl of Peterborough, in the war of the Spanish succession. Envoy Extraordinary and Minister Plenipotentiary at St. Petersburg in 1717. Repeatedly at the head of a fleet sent to the Baltic (*Dict. Nat. Biog.*, vol. xli., 1895).

the former in all points, and was better esteemed. Two ships, named the Ingermanland and Moscow, were launched at St. Petersburg. In autumn Captain Bredale, in the Samson, was despatched to cruise in the North Sea, and afterwards touch in England and Holland, and command the squadron, designed to be composed of the 3 new ships a-building in Holland, and 4 ships from Archangel expected to join him in Norway, and the Pearl, Oxford, Strafford, and St. Paul, ordered also for the North Seas. Of these, the St. Paul, Captain Batting, being very old, went no further than Copenhagen, and was broken up there; the Oxford proceeded to England, and never returned; the Pearl, Captain Griese, losing her mainmast, was obliged to put back and winter at Copenhagen: the Strafford, Captain Nahum Sinavin, reached Holland; and the Samson, Captain Bredale, was both in England and Holland. The commanders at Archangel with much difficulty got their ships launched, rigged, and over the bar in August; having likewise repaired and refitted, by the Tsar's directions, the Royal Transport yacht presented by his late Majesty King William to the Tsar, then in England. In September these 5, the Uriel, Captain Ivan Sinavin; Salafiel, Captain Bering; Varakiel, Captain Bents; Egudel, Captain Deane; and the Royal Transport, Captain Hutchisson, sailed in company from the bar at Arkhangel, in pursuance of their voyage to the Baltic; but the Egudel, springing a leak not to be repaired at sea, was ordered back to careen. The rest proceeding wintered—the Uriel and Salafiel at Copenhagen, the Varakiel at Flekkerö[1] in Norway, and the Royal Transport was cast away upon the coasts of Sweden: Captain Hutchisson saved and

[1] MS. 'Fleckery'; near Christiansand (*Norway Pilot*, 3rd ed.; 1897; i. p. 112).

made prisoner of war, with about 20 more, but is since dead in Marstrand[1] Castle. The Egudel, after careening and repairing, sailed from Archangel, and, passing the North Cape the last of November, with much ado got in and wintered about 25 leagues from Trondhjem, losing near half her men through the asperity of cold this season.

XII. PROCEEDINGS IN 1716.

Officers of all ranks were advanced this winter, and great preparations made at St. Petersburg and Revel; several ships laden with all manner of stores; and men-of-war, designed for the summer's expedition, ready to sail from Revel the first open water, to meet the rest of their fleet and join the Danes and other maritime Powers at Copenhagen. The Russ army was also to march thither, part by land and part on board the galleys; a project being formed in concert with the Danes to make a descent in Scania.[2] On the 20th of April, 1716, the squadron sailed from Revel under the command of Captain-Commodore Sievers, and, proceeding as far as Bornholm, received advice of the Swedish fleet consisting of 23 men-of-war lying before Copenhagen; and, holding a council of war, they took a resolution to go back, and arrived again at Revel by the 14th day of May. The Russ ships in the North Sea assembled at Flekkerö in Norway; whither came the Pearl, Captain Bering, to reinforce them, and they were joined by the Egudel, Captain Deane, on the last of April; as also in May by the Marlborough, Captain Bredale; the Devonshire, Captain Thofft; the Portsmouth, Captain Eckoff; the Strafford, Captain Sinavin; and the Samson, Captain Block; from Holland and England:

[1] MS. 'Masterland' (see *Norway Pilot*, i. p. 418).
[2] MS. 'Schonen,' the former Swedish province of Skåne.

Bredale commanding in chief. Three captains, several lieutenants and under-officers, lately engaged in the Tsar's service by Captain-Commodore Scheltinga, were on board these ships: but the major part of the under-officers and seamen, entertained by him and shipped in an hired vessel for Russia, receiving several months' pay in advance, mutinied; and 80 of them, getting ashore near the Texel in Holland, ran quite away. On the 27th of May this squadron sailed for Copenhagen, and anchored the 29th in the Sound; where then rode the British fleet under the command of the Honourable Sir John Norris, Admiral of the Blue. The Russ ships proceeded the next day to Copenhagen, and found the Uriel and Salafiel there. The beginning of June Captain Block, and one of the new officers, ordered in the Strafford down to Helsingör,[1] saluted there the British Admiral, striking his pennant at the same time, contrary to the Tsar's express prohibition on pain of death. It's affirmed he was drunk when he gave the orders; though being brought up in the Holland Navy, that always pays crowned heads this compliment, he might through indiscretion be guilty of this mistake. However, he was confined, and the winter following tried by a court-martial at Revel; and out of chagrin by excessive drinking shortened his days and died in confinement.

About this time Captain-Commodore Scheltinga came from Holland and took the command upon him, thereby redressing in some measure the disorders in the Russian fleet, before greatly embarrassed with the contending parties of Captain Bredale, Commander-in-Chief on the North Sea, and Captain Ivan Sinavin, that commanded [the] ships from Archangel. This last a sordid, drunken, ignorant fellow, a creature

[1] MS. 'Elseneur'; the Elsinore of *Hamlet* and of Campbell's ode.

of the Tsar's, and therefore of great power misused by him, to the exposing of himself and his Prince's service to ridicule. On the 7th of July the Tsar arrived with 37 sail of half-galleys, and a snow; the King of Denmark went off to compliment him aboard and, accompanying him in, received him in person ashore. On the 19th came into the Road the Russ squadron of 14 sail under Captain-Commodore Sievers, after a passage of 17 days from Revel; on the morrow the Tsar hoisting his flag on board the Ingermanland assumed the command as Vice-Admiral; and, saluted as such by all the fleet, went aboard the British Admiral, and was there magnificently entertained.

The Tsar made some alterations, assigning proper ships to select commanders; partly in regard to seniority, but more in respect to certain designs he had then in view. The new captains were placed in ships appointed to continue always in the fleet, on account of the unavoidable difficulties they must necessarily be involved in, through want of the languages wherein all officers in his service are obliged to command, viz. Russ, English, Hollands; and unacquaintance with the methods and customs, or, to speak more properly, the irregularity of their management. A commander here ought to have gone through all inferior posts, and be particularly well acquainted with the coasts and skilled in the art of navigation, since he is chargeable with and answerable for the duty of every officer under his command; whereas this science is little understood by the officers brought up in the Hollands Navy, the navigating part appertaining to the steersmen [1] as their peculiar province. This state of the case

[1] Persons belonging to the special pilotage or navigating branch of the service, and of various grades, as officers and petty-officers.

duly weighed may prevent any censure on this Prince's conduct in the frequent removal of his officers.

Matters adjusted to the best advantage, the Tsar, determining to send out in quest of the Swedish fleet, ordered Captains Baker of the Arundel, and Deane of the Samson, to wait upon the British Admiral and desire to know if he would appoint any cruisers; and if answered in the affirmative, to signify they had orders to join them: but Sir John Norris not thinking it proper to send any of his squadron, the Tsar commanded Deane in the Samson to find out the Swedes and bring him intelligence where they lay, as likewise of their number and force.

In pursuit of a stipulation between the Tsar and the King of Denmark, that which Prince soever present should command the forces of both nations by land or sea, the Tsar hoisted his standard; and being saluted by the British Admiral with 21 guns returned the salute with the same number. The Danes and Hollanders also saluted.

About the 5th they sailed. The British Admiral, with his squadron, some Dutch men-of-war, and a great fleet of merchants' ships under his care, sailed also in conjunction with them to Bornholm; and the Samson met them on the 8th with advice that the Swedes were gone into Karlskrona.[1]

The Strafford, Captain Lobanoff, was employed as a store-ship.

After some few days' stay the Tsar left his squadron in conjunction with the British and Danes, and went to the Island Rugen, from thence by Stralsund to Copenhagen.

By the beginning of September all the men-of-war, except the English and Dutch sent convoy up

---

[1] MS. 'Carlescrown.'

the Baltic, assembled in Copenhagen Roads; and now was the expected time to make the descent in Sweden; but it's foreign to this design to enter into a detail of the jealousies and misunderstandings that prevented the execution.

A LIST OF THE TSAR'S FLEET THEN PRESENT.

Flag Officers	Ships	Guns	Commanders
The Tsar . .	Ingermanland	64	Gosler
Captain-Commodore Scheltinga . .	Marlborough	70	Thosst
Captain-Commodore Sievers . .	Katharina	60	Laurence
—	Poltava	54	Van Gent
—	Portsmouth	60	Eckoff
—	Devonshire	60	Nahum Sinavin
—	St. Michael	52	Rue
—	St. Gabriel	52	Brant
—	Raphael	52	Huyck
—	Uriel	52	Ivan Sinavin
—	Salafiel	52	Bredale
—	Varakiel	52	Bents
—	Egudel	52	Vandergun
—	Fortune	48	Wessel
—	Pearl	52	Bering
—	Arundel	46	Baker
—	Lansdowne	40	Noble
—	Samson	32	Deane
—	Elias	28	Nelson
—	Princess (*snow*)	16	Muconoff
—	Natalia ,,	14	Schelling
—	Lesela ,,	14	Basheloff
—	Diana ,,	14	Harboe

The Tsar in the summer was heard to say he designed his frigates should winter at Kiel in Holstein and his ships of [the] line at Copenhagen; but the projected descent vanishing, he ordered his galleys and transports the beginning of October away for Mecklenburg, and sent the Arundel, Captain Baker, and the Samson, Captain Deane, to keep different courses up the Baltic, in order to countermand the store-ships then expected. Near Danzig they met the Slutelburg, Captain Edwards; the Moscow, Captain Besemacher; and the Victory, Captain Cramer, made a store-ship, with eight other vessels laden with stores and clothing for the army. These ships turned back, and soon after the Russian fleet under the command of the two Commodores returned from Copenhagen, the Tsar travelling by land into Holland. The Egudel, wanting some repairs, was obliged to stay at Copenhagen. Captain Bredale obtained leave of the Tsar to cruise in the snow Princess in the North Sea; it's thought, upon private intelligence of some Swedish ships trading under foreign colours. One snow was ordered to winter at Lübeck, to be subsisted ont of the contributions of Mecklenburg; and another at Danzig; the Tsar beginning about this time to form his pretensions on that city. The fourth, the Lesela, Captain Muconoff, was cast away upon Steffenshof, otherwise intended to winter at Rostock. The Princess was also lost on the coast of Jutland, the officers and most of the men saved; Bredale, thus disappointed, followed the Tsar to Holland and got an order to return to Copenhagen, and commanded the Egudel in pursuit of his project in the spring. Captain Vandergun, the former commander, upon a difference with the Ambassador, Prince Dolgoruki,[1] being destitute of a supply other ways, was obliged to dispose of some things belonging to the ship to buy bread for his people. This represented in an ill light to the Tsar by those who wanted his command, Bredale received orders to take him in

---

[1] Prince Vassili Vladimirovitz Dolgoruki, born 1667; died February 21, 1746 (A. Kleinschmidt, *Geschichte des russischen hohen Adels*, pp. 48, 50).

an arrest; and tried he was after near three years confinement; but, notwithstanding the court-martial—Captain-Commodore Sievers, President—acquitted him and allowed his accounts, yet not long since he was, and I fear still is, detained in soliciting justice; without the least subsistence afforded him since his first arresting, or any other regard had to the sentence in his favour, except his liberty, usually accompanying the court-martial's return of the sword.

The fleet taking in their way a small privateer of 4 guns, all arrived safe and wintered at Revel, it being too late to proceed to Kronslot; but this winter, before the bay of Revel was frozen up, a hard storm at north-north-west drove the sea with that violence against the new haven as destroyed it for several fathoms. Two ships, the Fortune and St. Antonio, were broken to pieces; and several others received much damage. In the fall of this year the Prince Alexander, pink, was launched at St. Petersburg. The Tsar being absent, few officers advanced this season, and no alterations worth taking notice of in the maritime affairs: all petitions receiving for answer, they must await the Tsar's return. The General-Admiral attended and gave general directions for the fleet to be in readiness, especially some frigates, against the spring. By the Tsar's orders were elected 72 youths from 16 to 20 years of age, heirs to about 100 roubles, or 25*l.* sterling p. ann. in villages or peasants; the customary way of computing estates there. These conducted to Revel, a commissary was appointed to provide for them at the Tsar's expense; and the 12th of April, the very day the ice broke up, they were all put on board the Samson, Captain Deane, that instantly sailed for Rostock, and, travelling thence into England and

Holland, they were bound apprentices, most of them for 5 years, to particular trades in those nations.

XIII. OPERATIONS OF 1717.

The Lansdowne, Captain Batting, sailed for Copenhagen, and the latter end of May arrived Mr. Paddon in character of Rear-Admiral of the White; and immediately by the General-Admiral's order hoisted his flag on board the Slutelburg. The beginning of July sailed the following squadron under the command of the General-Admiral :—

Flag Officers	Ships	Guns	Commanders
General - Admiral Apraxin and Captain - Commodore Sievers	Moscow	64	Hoogstraten
Rear - Admiral Paddon	Slutelburg	64	Huyck
Captain-Commodore Scheltinga	Marlborough	70	Armitage
—	Ingermanland	64	Gosler
—	Katharina	60	Besemacher
—	Portsmouth	60	Eckoff
—	Devonshire	60	Thofft
—	Poltava	54	Van Gent
—	Pearl	52	Van Hofft
—	St. Michael	52	Rue
—	Varakiel	52	Baker
—	Gabriel	52	Brant
—	Uriel	52	Turnhoud
—	Salafiel	52	Bering
—	Raphael	52	Nobel
—	Samson	32	Deane
—	Elias	28	Ducy

The[1] Le Firme, Randolph, L'Espérance and pink Alexander came also down from Kronslot to Revel.

[1] See note 1, p. 30.

When the General-Admiral approached Östergarn, on the north-east side of Gotland, he gave directions that the Portsmouth, Captain Eckoff, and the Samson, Captain Deane, as he came to anchor with the rest of the fleet, should keep under sail, and make the best of their way to Slitehamn,[1] about 6 leagues distant, and standing in near the fortifications observe their situation and force. At the fleet's going in to Östergarn, the Swedes from a few guns mounted fired some shot at the Russian Admiral, and then, nailing[2] their cannon and setting fire to their beacons, retired. The fleet anchored, and landed a considerable number of soldiers, more than half their complements being landmen. In the meantime the Portsmouth and Samson drawing near to Slitehamn, with a commanding gale of wind stood on and off within gun-shot of the fortification; sounding the depth of the water, and viewing its site and strength. This principally was on a small island disunited from the mainland by the passage into the harbour: they had also a large battery concealed by sticking green boughs resembling shrubs in the ground. The Russ ships made several shots to provoke the fire of the fort, the better to guess their force. When the Swedes perceived the Russ would not be decoyed nearer, they made a general fire from all their batteries at once, but with the aid of the gale the Russians sheered off, and returned to their fleet. Six days they continued at Östergarn with cruisers to the northward and southward, to give timely notice if the enemy's fleet should come out to attack them. Whilst they lay here the Poltava and Elias gave chase to a small privateer; the men to save themselves ran the vessel aground, and got the guns ashore to keep the Russ from getting her off. There

[1] MS. 'Slighthaven.' [2] *I.e.* spiking.

was not depth of water for the ships to approach, so 2 boats went aboard; and in the confusion, instead of attempting to bring her off, contented themselves only to set her on fire, and retreated: the Swedes immediately descending extinguished it; and the Poltava, returning to the fleet, left the Elias to prevent the privateer's escape. When Captain Van Gent of the Poltava gave in this report it extremely incensed the General-Admiral; so that calling to him Captain Deane, of the Samson, that moment come aboard to make a report of his cruise to the southward, he bid him take what ships or vessels he should have occasion for and fetch away the privateer: or, if not to be done, to burn her as she lay; and, driving off the people, to bring away her guns and what else came to hand: upon his return he would give him a handsome reward. The Samson took 2 long boats and as many pinnaces, manned and armed; but coming to the place found the Elias had let the privateer escape.

The fleet departed from Gotland, having taken good store of great and small cattle, and but little else of value, leaving the houses undemolished. By the latter end of July they arrived at Revel, where the General-Admiral held a court-martial over the officers of the Poltava and Elias with a resolution to cashier[1] them all: but the court thought fit to dismiss the Captain, and break the Lieutenant of the Elias only. The General-Admiral struck his flag, and went into the country for a few days, giving the charge of the fleet to Rear-Admiral Paddon, with directions to go out and exercise them in forming lines of battle; but this attempt ended in confusion and dispute. The Pearl, Portsmouth, and pink Alexander sailed a-cruising, and in a short time brought in a Swedish snow of 16 guns; Captain

---

[1] MS. 'cashire.'

Van Hofft, of the Pearl, and Captain Chapezan, of the pink Alexander, contesting whose prize she was. Rear-Admiral Paddon sailed on the 27th of August with 11 of the best ships for Kronslot to winter there. The Lansdowne and New Kronslot of 16 guns, built in Holland, arrived from Copenhagen where the Egudel, Captain Bredale, continued this winter. In September the Ormonde, Captain Blorey, richly laden on the Tsar's account and bound to Venice, sailed in company with the British convoy through the Baltic. The Tsar returning from abroad took a view of the haven at Revel, now greatly improved, and the same was further enlarged this season. Some English merchant ships, too late for their convoy, applying to the Tsar, he ordered the Uriel and Samson to conduct them as far as Danzig: they put out to sea in October, but at last were forced back and obliged to winter at Revel. The St. Alexander, Neptunus, and Revel were launched this fall at St. Petersburg; where the Academy set on foot some years ago for the education of Guardmarines, or young gentlemen Reformadoes[1] designed for the Navy, met more than usual encouragement and success: the confiscated house of Alexander Kikin,[2] late Admiraliteits Heer, executed as an accomplice in the Tsarovitz's affair, being appropriated to that use. Messieurs Ferguson and

---

[1] Perhaps these persons were supernumerary to certain corps in the land forces. 'Reformado, or *reformed officer*, one whose troop or company is suppressed in a *reform*, and he continued in the whole or half pay, doing duty in the regiment. A *reformed* Captain of foot follows the company, and assists the standing officer as a second; but he still maintains his degree and precedence' (E. Chambers, F.R.S., *Cyclopædia*, 1750, vol. ii.). See *post*, p. 113.

[2] According to Herrmann (iv. p. 324) Kikin, though twice knouted, was not at first put to death. All his property was confiscated, and they 'left him nothing but his shirt and coat.' He was subsequently executed.

Gwyn, masters in the mathematics of a considerable standing at Moscow, were removed and settled here. A new officer, under the name of Secretary, was appointed for each ship, to rank with a lieutenant, and his instructions directed him to inspect into the conduct of all officers, go with the first boats on board all prizes, take an inventory and seal up all things of value, keep books of expenses of all stores, and particularly observe all that the captain brought into or took out of the ship. Also now came up the custom of having lads to serve as cabin boys in the fleet, and so be trained up for seamen.

The Tsar, when last in Holland, engaged in his service Captains-Commodores Gordon and Saunders, Captain Hay and Captain-Lieutenants Urquhart and Serocold; these with 2 land officers, all Britons, arrived this winter. The Strafford was converted into an hospital ship; and several cruisers got ready in the port of Revel to sail the first open water. The new haven at Kronslot carried on with all possible expedition; and the dock and basin designed. A canal of communication betwixt the rivers Volhoff and Neva, of 70 miles extent, for accommodating the city of St. Petersburg with the produce of the country at cheaper rates, by water carriage, was also resolved upon, and Captain-Lieutenant Van Werden, with several others, was sent to Astracan to make discoveries on the Caspian Sea.

XIV. EVENTS IN 1718.

On New Year's Day, according to custom, several officers were advanced; particularly Prince Menshikoff from Rear-Admiral of the Red to Rear-Admiral of the Blue; and Captain-Commodore Scheltinga to Rear-Admiral of the Red. The raising of Scheltinga to a flag at this juncture was matter of much speculation; since all knew his ill success in his late commission of engaging officers in the Tsar's service in Holland; which cost that Prince very dear. Moreover, for a year past and upwards, he had lost the use of one side by a paralytic infirmity; the most probable conjecture is the Tsar, thinking he could not live long, was willing to grant him the honour of dying Rear-Admiral. The 3 ships launched in autumn were equipped this spring, and the fleet got ready; but no great preparations made on the part of the galleys. On the side of Finland it had the air of a cessation of arms; and the Tsar's ordering Baron Görtz,[1] in November last, to be transported from Revel to Helsingfors, from whence he travelled to Sweden, could not but produce a general whisper of peace.

The cruisers at Revel had orders to sail as soon as ever the ice broke up; not to molest any Swedish ships with General Bruce's[2] passports; and to open their private instructions when 20 leagues in sea.[3] Accordingly on the 8th of May, 1718, sailed the Pearl, Captain Van Hofft; Uriel, Captain Turnhoud; Randolph, Captain Bents; Samson, Captain Deane; St. Jacob, Captain Lobanoff; and the Diana snow, Captain Arseenoff. Arriving at the

[1] 'Le fameux baron de Görtz, le plus délié et le plus entreprenant des hommes, d'un esprit vaste et fécond en ressources' (Voltaire, 'Hist. de Russie sous Pierre le Grand,' Œuvres, vol. xvi. p. 547). Georg Heinrich Görtz, Baron von Schlitz, called Von Görtz. Born 1668; executed March 13, 1719. At first in the service of Duke of Holstein-Gottorp, and afterwards of Charles XII. of Sweden. As a negotiator and diplomatic intriguer he occupies a large space in Voltaire's works on Charles XII. and Russia. After Charles's death he was tried at Stockholm and put to death (*Allgemeine Deutsche Biographie*, vol. ix.; Leipzig, 1879).
[2] General Jacob Daniel Bruce, A.D.C. to Peter the Great, one of the Russian plenipotentiaries who signed the treaty of Nystadt, $\frac{\text{August 30}}{\text{September 10}}$ 1721.
[3] The phrase 'in sea' occurs more than once.

directed distance, they unsealed their orders and found that the Uriel and Randolph were to cruise in that station; the Pearl and Samson to proceed, and cruise at large on the enemy's coast, to hinder all trade with Sweden, and make prize of all nations, French and Hollanders excepted; the St. Jacob and snow Diana to go to Danzig, and reinforce the Russ already there in obstructing all commerce betwixt that city and Sweden.

This month the Egudel, Captain Bredale, arrived from Copenhagen, with Rear-Admiral Paddon's family aboard, and one Mr. Little made a captain by the Tsar soon after his landing. In June the fleet fitted out at Kronslot sailed for Revel, under the command of Vice-Admiral Peter Alexeievitz, the Tsar; but Rear-Admiral Scheltinga died before its departure. In the meantime the Pearl and Samson cruising, sometimes in company sometimes apart, made prize of, and sent into the port of Revel, several ships bound to and from Sweden. Captains Stegman and Bohen, 2 lieutenants, and about 50 under-officers and seamen, entertained in the Tsar's service by his residence at Hamburg, travelling by and through Poland, arrived at Revel. Captain Bents, in the Randolph, was sent to Hamburg, to bring the fine yacht formerly presented by the States of Holland to the King of Prussia; and now given by that prince to the Tsar. The latter end of June came in the Pearl and Samson with four prizes more; 2 whereof the Samson had fetched out of Burgs Vik harbour in Gotland passing for a Swede, and amusing the people on the batteries with Swedes' colours and friendly discourse, till he had accomplished his purpose. After 3 days' stay they sailed again a-cruising. The fleet from Kronslot continuing a few days at Revel, proceeded to Råger Wik, and thence to Hangö Head. The

Tsar this summer took a resolution to form a haven at Råger Wik, but deferred the execution of his design till peace. However, he built a house for himself, and erected a cross, railed in to prohibit any profane access.

The ships were employed in various stations, and on different affairs; so that they were assembled together all this summer: and the major part were not 3 days at a time out of harbour. The Le Firme received some damage, and, being old and crazy, was ordered back to Kronslot, and never went to sea again. The Dumcraft, Standard, St. Nicholas, Pernau, Richmond, and Gabriel were also condemned as unfit for service. The Pearl and Samson, still a-cruising, sent in several prizes more to Revel. The Samson chasing a Swedes privateer into a narrow creek, inaccessible to the frigate, the privateer's people got 4 guns ashore, with intention to defend their vessel from any further injury: but the Samson coming near enough to drive them with her cannon from their battery, they set their ship on fire and retreated; the Russians landing in their pinnace brought off their guns, ammunition, and what else they could preserve from the flames. The beginning of August the Pearl and Samson returned to Revel, and refitting sailed upon the third cruise. The pink Alexander also continued cruising; and the St. Michael and Varakiel were sent on different errands to Danzig. This month the squadron designed for Kronslot sailed thither; and the ships appointed to winter at Revel were left under the command of Captain-Commodore Saunders. Several prizes were sent in by the Pearl and Samson; and in September arrived the ships from Danzig, with all the cruisers. Nothing more of moment interven'd this summer except the retaking of two of the prizes by Swedish cruisers; and

A List of the Ships in Motion this Year

Flag Officers	Ships	Guns	Commanders
Vice-Admiral Peter Alexeievitz, the Tsar	Ingermanland	64	Gosler
Rear-Admiral of the White, Paddon	Slutelburg	64	Little
Rear-Admiral of the Blue, Prince Menshikoff	St. Alexander	70	Brant
Captain-Commodore Sievers	Neptunus	70	Hoogstraten
Captain-Commodore Gordon	Katharina	60	Laurence
Captain-Commodore Saunders	Marlborough	70	Delap
—	Revel	60	Ivan Sinavin
—	Moscow	64	Falkenberg
—	Portsmouth	60	Eckoff
—	Devonshire	60	Thofft
—	Egudel	52	Bredale
—	Le Firme	70	Wessel
—	Randolph	52	Bents
—	London	52	Chapezan
—	Britannia	52	Batting
—	Pearl	52	Van Hofft
—	Uriel	52	Turnhoud
—	Varakiel	52	Hay
—	St. Michael	52	Stegman
This ship thoroughly repaired	Riga	52	Nahum Sinavin
—	Samson	32	Deane
—	Elias	28	Vianen
—	*pink*, Alexander	24	Armitage
Being old and crazy, altered from 40 to 24 guns	Lansdowne	24	Tressel
—	St. Jacob	16	Lobanoff
—	*snows* { Diana	14	Arseenoff
—	*snows* { Natalia	14	Bashelloff

the recovery of one again by the Russ. Likewise the Governor of Pillau kept under arrest 2

Russian officers, by way of reprisal, for 2 captures made by their cruisers in sight of the castle. An English and Dutch man-of-war retook from the Russ two prizes, belonging to their respective nations: and some disputes happened, on the article of salutes, with the Hollands ships of war. In autumn were launched the Lesnoy and Hangö Head, so named in memory of the actions at Lesnoy in Poland and Hangö Head in Finland, where Rear-Admiral Ehrenskiöld was taken. Early in the winter died Rear-Admiral Paddon, and was succeeded on New Year's Day by Prince Menshikoff as Rear-Admiral of the White; Captain-Commodore Sievers made Rear-Admiral of the Blue, and Captain-Commodore Gordon Rear-Admiral of the Red.

XV. NAVAL ADMINISTRATION AND PROCEEDINGS IN 1719.

Sievers, now advanced, was born at Copenhagen, and served the King of Denmark in his Navy about the year 1708; engaging in the Tsar's service as captain, he was sometimes employed on board, sometimes in the yard, as Under-Equipage Master;[1] something at that time resembling our Master Attendant and Storekeeper united. He is a man of excellent sense, general knowledge and very exact and methodical in all his conduct; speaks and writes most European tongues; many Russians of distinction will assure you, not a man of their own nation understands their language so well as he. These qualifications render him of great importance; besides he is a bold man; and during the time the ships lie in harbour, in dividing the officers and men, &c., has refused to suffer Rear-Admiral Gordon to be present

---

[1] See *ante*, note 9, p. 5.

at the opening, or consulted upon the execution of orders; even when desired by the Tsar. It is thought that Prince esteems Gordon before him; but he is highly in the good graces of the General-Admiral, his professed peculiar patron.

Something being represented to the disadvantage of Captain Bents, of the Randolph, then wintering at Hamburg, Captain Nahum Sinavin was dispatched by land to command that ship, and as he found the case so to use his former commander.

The Tsar, for several years past having obliged all shipbuilders to take young men and teach them their art, now ordered several builders' assistants to be dismissed : Hadley, Davenport and Ramsey being raised to master builders. The Admiralty [1] College, as well as 8 others of different Institution, at St. Petersburg, having been for some time gradually advancing, now began to act with full power. The Members that sat constantly during the winter, except two days in the week wherein the President took his place in the Senate, were :

General-Admiral Count [2] Apraxin, President; Vice-Admiral Cruys, Vice-President; Vice-Admiral Peter Alexeievitz, the Tsar. Occasionally General Charnishoff, Commissary of War and Intendant de Marine.

Colonel Norroff, for clothing of Sailors and all Contracts.

Secretary Tormeshoff.

---

[1] These 'colleges'—a word which in this connection is equal to our 'boards'—were the several Ministries or Public Offices amongst which the administration of the affairs of the Empire was distributed by Peter the Great. His *Ukase* establishing them is dated December 12, 1718. They are described by Herrmann (*Gesch. Russ. Staates*, iv. pp. 381-5). The Admiralty College, corresponding to our Board of Admiralty, was composed of at least seven members chosen from naval officers not serving afloat. The General-Admiral also was a member.

[2] MS. 'Graff.'

This college has the charge of paying, victualling and providing stores for the fleet; issuing all orders to the flag officers and particular ships; confirming and publishing the proceedings of courts-martial, and everything else of moment, when ratified by the Tsar; but if he is absent, copies of all transactions are transmitted to him; and nothing of consequence determined till they receive the sanction of his approbation. Midshipmen were this winter established in the Navy; and more than ordinary application used to have the men-of-war and galleys in readiness. The Army was quartered in adjacent places to embark at the seaports the first open water, in order to accelerate the peace with Sweden. Due preparations were also made at Revel for the cruisers to be early out; in the meantime great disputes arose at this port about the command betwixt Captain-Commodore Saunders and Captain Van Hofft, lately made commodore; till at last the college ordered Commodore Saunders away to command a ship at St. Petersburg. Orders came to Revel by Lieutenant Count Nicolas Golovin[1] to have completely provided, besides the frigates for cruising, three transports with 40 soldiers each, over and above their proper complement; and this lieutenant to accompany the cruisers in what ship he pleased, having in his custody the instructions that were to be opened at sea. About the latter end of April, 1719, arrived the Randolph, Captains Sinavin and Bents, with the transport yacht from Hamburg, as also the Ormonde, Captain Blorey, from Venice, having wintered in Norway.

[1] Count Nikolaï Feodorovitz Golovin, Envoy at Stockholm, Admiral and President of the Admiralty College. In 1741 summoned to the Council by the Empress Elizabeth. In May, 1743, commanded a squadron against the Swedes. Died at Hamburg, May 6, 1745 (Kleinschmidt, *Ges. russ. hohen Adels*, p. 168).

The ice pretty well gone and the cruisers hauled out, sailed the Pearl, Captain-Commodore Van Hofft; Samson, Captain Deane; pink Alexander, Captain Tressel; Elias, Captain Vianen; and the Lansdown, Captain Count [1] Apraxin. Arriving at the directed station they opened their orders commanding them to obstruct as much as possible all trade to and from Sweden, by making prize of all nations trafficking thither, without exception; the transports to wear Lübeck colours,[2] and, taking a favourable opportunity of wind and weather, to come to an anchor in an evening under the Swedish shore, as near Karlskrona as they could conveniently; whilst the cruisers—keeping out of sight by day, all but one, to observe and give notice where the transports anchored—were, as soon as it was dark, to stand in sufficiently near and send their boats well manned and armed to the transports, and from thence in concert land and bring off what people of fashion should fall in their way, in order to get intelligence of the real state of the Swedish fleet; and, by an alarm given on this side, facilitate the intended descent in a different quarter. When the cruisers were arrived near the spot for executing this design, a consultation was held, Count Golovin present; the orders mentioning that he, though but a lieutenant, should sit in all councils and expressly appointing him to command the present descent, the superior officers perceived the Tsar's intention in so positively directing he should command, was to give him an occasion to signalise himself in order to [further] his future advancement. However, he seemed diffident, and desired some expedient might be used to learn whether soldiers were

---

[1] MS. 'Graff.'
[2] Carried by Lübeck ships till 1866. The flag was half white, half red, horizontal.

cantoned in the villages along the coasts or not. The design was waived; the Samson was despatched upon a three days' cruise for intelligence, and at the expiration of the time returned with three good prizes, and several passengers aboard. A second consultation was held, and the passengers examined; still nothing could be done as to landing. Again the Samson was ordered out for three days, with the Lansdowne under her command, to cruise near the mouth of the river [1] of Stockholm, if possible to intercept the post-yacht statedly passing betwixt that city and Visby. In seven days' cruise they took fourteen prizes, and on board one of them Monsieur Van Merch, Privy Councillor to the King of Prussia, who had been both at Karlskrona and Stockholm and very well knew the state of affairs. In returning to the rest of the cruisers they were taken with a very hard gale of wind; so that the prizes unable to keep the sea and the two frigates, after manning so many vessels destitute of sufficient hands, were all obliged in this condition to bear away for Revel. On their safe arrival there a courier was despatched to the Tsar, it not being known but the General-Admiral had sailed. Captain Deane, having got all the prizes into the haven, and committed Monsieur Van Merch to the care of Count Apraxin, commander of the Lansdowne, with orders to await the return of the courier, and know the Tsar's pleasure, sailed after two days' stay on the 21st of May. The Tsar sent a coach with an officer of his Guards to bring Mr. Van Merch to Kronslot, and, after gaining what intelligence he could, in a few days gave him leave to depart.

On the 18th sailed from Revel, a-cruising, the Portsmouth, Captain Nahum Sinavin; Devonshire, Captain Zotoff; Egudel, Captain Delap; Uriel,

[1] The inlet or fiord.

Captain Turnhoud; Varakiel, Captain Stegman; Raphael, Captain Chapezan; and snow Diana, Captain Lopakin. This squadron engaged and took a ship of 44 guns, another of 28, and a snow of 12, sent out in quest of the Samson and Lansdowne. The day the news arrived a ship was to be launched and named the Isaak, but the Tsar upon this success called her the Isaak Victoria. The Pearl and other cruisers had also taken several prizes. By the 2nd of June the cruisers in general were returned to Revel, where they had orders to wait the arrival of the fleet from Kronslot under the command of Vice-Admiral Peter Alexeievitz, whose departure had been retarded some days by the following accident. The ship Lesnoy, Rear-Admiral Gordon and Captain Batting commanders, built by the Tsar himself, and drawing 22 feet water, as she was towing out of the haven, where is at most but 24 feet, came upon the fluke[1] of an anchor, that ran through her bottom, and she bilged and sank. This misfortune much chagrined the Tsar; however, at last leaving directions with Prince Menshikoff and Captain Lane, his chief engineer at Kronslot, to use all possible efforts to weigh her up, he sailed with the fleet and arrived the 20th of June at Revel. Prize-money was distributed amongst the ships concerned in the late action with the three Swedes; Nahum Sinavin made Captain-Commodore, and some other commanding officers advanced for that service. On the 23rd, after some alteration in the appointment of the officers, the whole fleet sailed from Revel, and the 27th put into Hangö Head, where the General-Admiral lay with the galleys. Several cruisers were sent out, particularly the Samson, Captain Zotoff, and the New Kronslot, Captain Count Golovin, to observe the motion of the British[2] squadron. On the

[1] MS. 'fflook.'   [2] Under Adm. Sir John Norris.

2nd of July, the Tsar striking his flag, resigned the command to Rear-Admiral Sievers, and went on board the galleys. The fleet sailed from Hangö Head the 3rd of July, and the next day two small Danish frigates joined them ; the Princes of the North being jealous of each other at this crisis, the Russians looked upon these Danes as spies. The Tsar went before to Åland in the galleys, as also several officers of the men-of-war, to make observations, fix beacons, and be ready to pilot in the fleet, which drawing near to the shore on the 8th of this month, the pilots came off and conducted it into Rödhamn, a good harbour under Lemland ; the same day Vice-Admiral Peter Alexeievitz went aboard and hoisted his flag.

These ships composed the united Russian Fleet, though generally four or five of them were out a-cruising. The latter end of the month the Hangö Head was ordered up to Kronslot, and convoyed as far as Revel by two men-of-war. The reason was she could bear no sails if it blowed anything hard ; and twice her masts have been reduced to remedy this inconvenience. Rear-Admiral Sievers went on board the St. Alexander. Some Russian cruisers always kept a good way in sea, in order to give timely notice of the enemy ; as also to inform the Samson and New Kronslot where the fleet lay, should they come with advice of the motion of the British Squadron.

The men-of-war now safe in harbour and cruisers appointed on every side, the General-Admiral having assembled the greatest part of his army, the Great Chancellor Count Golovkin,[1] and the Vice-Chancel-

---

[1] Gavrila Ivanovitz Golovkin ; born March, 1660; died January 30, 1734 ; Chancellor of the Empire, 1709 ; created Count, 1710 (A. Kleinschmidt, *Ges. des russischen hohen Adels*, p. 337).

A List of the Russian Fleet lying at Anchor under Lemland in line of Battle.

Flag Officers	Ships	Guns	Commanders
—	Katharina	60	Bredale
—	Arundel	46	Muconoff
—	Uriel	52	Turnhoud
Rear-Admiral Sievers	Hanghoud	90	Falkenberg
Captain-Commodore Van Hofft	Marlborough	70	Kasheloff
—	Egudel	52	Delap
—	Devonshire	60	Deane
Reduced to this number of guns	Raphael	40	Chapezan
—	Pearl	52	Villebois
Captain-Commodore Saunders	Neptunus	70	Masnoy
Vice-Admiral Peter Alexeievitz	Ingermanland	64	Gosler
—	St. Alexander	70	Brant
—	Varakiel	52	Stegman
—	Randolph	52	Bents
—	Salafiel	52	Bering
Captain-Commodore Sinavin	Portsmouth	60	Urquhart
—	Britannia	50	Lenoy
Rear-Admiral Gordon	Moscow	64	Hay
—	Slutelburg	64	Wessel
—	London	52	Little
—	Revel	64	Ivan Sinavin

lor Baron Schaffiroff,[1] being present, a grand council of war was held, and debates arising, the Tsar ordered his ministers, generals, and flag-officers to deliver in writing the next morning their sentiments concerning the intended descent. This

[1] The first person to be created a Russian Baron. He was a Jew named Schaffer, who became a Christian and was given the name of Peter Schaffiroff by Peter the Great. Baron in 1710; Vice-Chancellor in 1711. Knouted and sentenced to be beheaded in 1723; he was pardoned and died in March 1739.

obeyed, the following day the General-Admiral with the galleys left the ships of war; and, rowing within the rocks till they reached the narrowest place about six or seven leagues wide, crossed over to the Swedish shore, under convoy of six men-of-war, commanded by Captain-Commodore Sinavin. The fame of their depredations [1] being spread far and near, supersedes any farther relation; all I shall presume to say is, the Tsar's commands were positive, and performed with reluctance by the Commander-in-Chief. The Generals under the High Admiral were Buturlin,[2] Galitzin,[3] and Lesley;[4] the

---

[1] 'Les Russes rasèrent 8 villes, 141 maisons de nobles, 1361 villages et 43 moulins. Ils détruisirent 2 mines de cuivre, 14 usines et 16 magasins; ils tuèrent 100000 bestiaux, jetèrent dans la mer 80000 barres de fer, et mirent en partant le feu à une forêt de 80 lieues d'étendue, pour détruire les mines de cuivre et de fer qu'on y exploitait.' (Depping's note to Levesque's *Histoire de Russie*, ed. 1812, vol. v. p. 75.) Herrmann (*Geschichte des russischen Staates*, vol. iv. pp. 338–9) gives slightly different figures. He adds that many young people and children and a large number of copper-wire makers were carried off to St. Petersburg.

[2] Ivan Ivanovitz Buturlin, Lieut.-Colonel of the 2nd Regiment of Preobrojensky Guards. In 1700, as a Major-General, he commanded the 1st Division of the Army. On November 30, 1700, he was taken prisoner at the battle of Narva; was afterwards set free and made Lieutenant-General. He was arrested, degraded, and banished to his estates in 1727 (Kleinschmidt, pp. 187–8).

[3] Prince Michaïl Michaïlovitz Galitzin; born November 1675; died December 1730. For his bravery at the capture of Nöteburg made Colonel of the Semenoff Regiment of Guards; Major-General, 1708; Lieut.-General, 1709; Governor-General of Russian Finland in 1714. In 1725 made Field-Marshal-General (Kleinschmidt, p. 889).

[4] Though the name in the MS. is Lesley, as retained in the text, it is probable that it was really Lacy. Peter Lacy, afterwards Count and Russian Field-Marshal, was born at Killeedy, co. Limerick, September 29 (O.S.), 1678. At a very early age he took part in the defence of Limerick. Left Ireland with Sarsfield's troops, and served in the Irish Brigade of France. Entered the Russian Service. Colonel,

last, an Irish papist, always commanded apart with his division, and perpetrated innumerable devastations. During the continuance of the fleet at Rödhamn, a detachment of sailors and part of the army that stayed behind were employed in fortifying the entrance into the haven ; and the 2 prahms, with the bomb-ketches, were directed to post themselves there, whilst several boats and pinnaces were set to find out other channels, whereby the fleet might retreat in case of necessity. On the 18th of August the Tsar sent to recall the galleys, and then returned on the 20th in the night; the next day, after taking leave of his officers in a friendly manner, thanking them for their good services, and recommending observance to Rear-Admiral Sievers' orders, he struck his flag and went on board the galleys in order to go back to Kronslot. Immediately Rear-Admiral Sievers with the fleet under his command sailed out by another channel, having in company several merchant ships of different nations, taken either in the Swedish harbours or on their coasts, and arrived on the 24th at Revel. Captain Villebois meanwhile with two snows made the best of his way to Danzig. On the 25th came in the New Kronslot with advice ; whereupon a consultation was held, and the two flags with the Kronslot Squadron weighing stood out and anchored under the Isle of Nargen, in readiness to sail, if the British fleet, now daily expected, should come in sight. Cruisers were likewise kept constantly out to watch their approach, and fire beacons, affixed on all the points of land,

---

1708 ; Major-General, 1712 ; Lieut.-General, 1720 ; Field-Marshal, 1736. 'He signalised himself in the war by his many descents on the Swedish coast.' Served under the Empresses Ann and Elizabeth, and died $\frac{\text{April 30}}{\text{May 11}}$, 1751 (*Dict. Nat. Biog.*, vol. xxxi.). The name is often spelled Lascy by Continental writers.

from Kotka[1] Island to Kronslot, to give speedy notice of their appearance. The import of the New Kronslot's intelligence being sent to the Tsar, orders came from the flags to sail with their squadron to Kronslot; and the rest of the ships to remain in Revel haven. All due preparations made and everybody in expectation of the British and Swedish fleets at Revel or Kronslot, or both, on the 22nd of September, Adjutant-General Rumanzoff[2] came express from the Tsar with directions for the three best ships to get in their guns and sail for Kronslot with all possible expedition. This was executed in much hurry and confusion; and the 25th sailed the London, Captain Little; the Devonshire, Captain Deane; and the Portsmouth, Captain Urquhart; and on the 29th, within 5 leagues of Kronslot, the London and Portsmouth both running on a sandbank, the Devonshire came to an anchor, and, sending to the commanding officer at Kronslot for help, assisted with his boats and people: the captains consulted and did all that lay in their power to get the ships off; but the weather proving bad, no assistance coming from Kronslot, and all their pinnaces and boats being lost, they resolved to cut away their masts; in performance whereof the Captain of the Portsmouth was killed, and the ships soon after bilged. On the 1st of October Captain Deane, having his officers on board the two ships, and no boat left, was obliged to cut his cable and run up to

[1] MS. 'Otkins Holme,' which appears to be the Kotka (or Rotchen Salm) Island of *The Baltic Pilot*, Part II.
[2] Alexander Ivanovitz Rumanzoff, son of a small landed proprietor in the province of Kostroma; born 1684; died March 15, 1749. In 1708 entered the Preobrojensky Guards as a private soldier. Became Captain. Discovered the fugitive Alexeï and brought him back to Moscow in 1718. Adjutant-General in the Northern war. Served later against the Turks. Created Count by the Empress Elizabeth in 1744.

Kronslot to save the Devonshire. The first news brought to the Tsar at St. Petersburg was of one ship running aground only; but coming down to Kronslot he learnt the whole truth to his great aggravation. Nor were there wanting some to censure the Captain that had preserved his ship; alleging he had served the Tsar many years, was well acquainted with the coasts, and known to be none of the best of friends with Captain Little, that commanded at that time; whereas the other two Captains were of late standing in the Tsar's service and of little experience in those seas. But it appeared, upon examination, that the two ships lost were near 2 miles ahead of the Devonshire; and that about half an hour before they ran aground, the Captain of the Devonshire ordered his officers to keep a different course. But, 'tis thought, the Tsar always imputed this loss to party emulation; whereas the real cause was Captain Little's ignorance and too much pride to ask advice. The Tsar appointed a court-martial upon the officers of the two ships, Prince Menshikoff President; wherein Captain Little was condemned to 6 months' confinement and afterwards to serve as youngest lieutenant: and the mate of his ship to the galleys.[1] A great deal of pains was taken and a variety of means used to retrieve these ships; but all in vain. The Tsar, resolving to keep the number of his ships of [the] line, ordered the Poltava, sent up to St. Petersburg to be rebuilt, to be brought back to Kronslot and equipped with officers and men appointed as if designed to accompany the fleet in case it went to sea: but being entirely unfit, an attempt of this kind must have proved of the last ill

---

[1] Either removed from the Navy and appointed to the Galley Fleet—which was a subordinate service; or sentenced to the oar as a convict or galley slave—a common punishment at the time.

consequence. The Lesnoy was weighed up by Captain Lane; and two ships launched, one named the Fredrikstadt, from a place in Holstein, where the Russian troops behaved well; the other Severnoi Oril (or the Northern Eagle).

For two years past the Tsar's creatures had used some address to sound the inclinations of the foreign officers he esteemed; if possible to induce them to [? sign] Articles of Service for life. One or two suspected of contracting privately in this kind received several favours by way of encouragement and for an allurement to others. This was now more openly proposed, the Tsar himself in his cups frequently toasting: 'A Health to all brave officers, that never design to leave me; especially during the war!' obliquely reflecting on some particular commanders that refused all offers and peremptorily insisted upon a dismission. Foreigners belonging to the Colleges [1] were proved in like manner; but generally rejected the temptation: only such as were Swedes born were compelled to a compliance.

The Katharine, Moscow, and Ingermanland, though built of oak timber, were observed to be much destroyed: this was imputed in part to their lying in fresh water in Kronslot, and partly to a putrifying damp, caused by the extreme hard frost in the winter, that greatly impaired the timber and plank within board, especially betwixt wind and water. To prevent this inconvenience for the future, the Tsar ordered holes to be cut two foot above the water's edge, afore and abaft, to give the air a free passage betwixt the ships' sides and the ceiling.

The Tsar having procured the *Articles of War*, and the *Regulations* of the Navies of England, France, Holland, Denmark, and Sweden, with

[1] See note 1, p. 62.

officers experienced in the methods of those nations, resolved to examine them with the greatest accuracy in order to select such parts as should be most subservient to his purpose. Accordingly a Board was established in his own Banqueting House, where he himself constantly attended by 4 o'clock in the morning. The other members were Rear-Admiral Gordon, Captain-Commodore Oto, Master of the Naval Ordnance, Captains Gosler, Zotoff, Mishecoff, and occasionally the General-Admiral Apraxin and Rear-Admiral Sievers. These had also recourse, for their further instruction, to sundry Treatises of different nations; particularly *de Jure Maritimo*, taught several years ago to speak[1] the Russian language.

The Tsar, when in France, engaged in his service an engineer[2] that undertook to haul up any ships upon the dry land; a performance of infinite difficulty in those parts, because there is neither ebb nor flood. The[3] Le Firme, brought up to the yard in autumn, was appointed to undergo the experiment; a vast

---

[1] 'Taught to speak' is in the MS. Perhaps in the original draft the word was 'brought.' The phrase—as meaning 'translated into Russian'—was probably archaic even in 1724. Mr. J. E. Matthew, in his *Handbook of Musical History*, London, 1898, p. 83, gives the title of an early collection of madrigals as follows: '*Musica Transalpina* : Madrigales of foure, five, and sixe parts, chosen out of divers excellent Authors, with the first and second part of *La Verginella*, made by Maister Byrd upon two stanz's of Ariosto, and brought to speak English with the rest,' &c. The date is London, 1588.

The work alluded to was, perhaps, *De Jure Maritimo et Navali, a Treatise of Affairs Maritime and of Commerce*; by Charles Molloy, 1682: republished 1701.

In Zedler's *Lexikon*, vol. xxxvi. (1743), mention is made of several treatises *de Jure Maritimo* published in the 17th and early part of the 18th centuries. At the date indicated in the text the most recent of these seems to have been *Brevis Introductio in Notitiam Legum Nauticarum et Scriptorum Juris Reique Maritimæ*; Lübeck, 1713, attributed to Andreas Lange.

[2] MS. 'ingenier.'

[3] See note 1, p. 30.

quantity of cordage, blocks and other requisite materials were provided; and several thousand men employed. At length the attempt succeeded at the expense of near two months' labour, about 80[1] tons of cordage, and the mangling, maiming, and killing outright of many poor people. The Frenchman likewise, unaccustomed to so cold a climate, got his death in attending the project; leaving a ship unfinished that was a-building under his direction.

The outworks at Kronslot were carried on this winter with the utmost vigour, and a boom consisting of huge baulks, joined together with cramp irons, large iron chains, and great cables, was fixed between the two pier[2] heads, across the passage into the harbour. Three old ships were also prepared to be sunk in the entrance into the haven, with beams fixed in them to facilitate their weighing again; and a great quantity of stones lay ready to be distributed, in nets capable of receiving about fifty or sixty pounds weight each, in order to be thrown into the ships to keep them upright at and after their immersion; one end of a line, fastened to each net, being to be secured above water, to draw up the stones again with ease whenever they intended to haul up the ships.

XVI. EVENTS IN 1720.

As soon as the ice was gone in 1720, cruisers were kept out at sea at equal distances [apart], to receive and transfer the proper signal, in case of the approach of an enemy; being the more apprehensive of an insult, because the new works were unfortified. No less also were their expectations of the enemy at Revel, whither Major-General Gouter of the Artillery was despatched to put everything in good order and continue there. As they conjectured the British

---

[1] MS. 'tun.'   [2] MS. 'peer.'

admiral would make some overtures of mediation, orders were sent to all the governors of seaports, and to the commanding officer of the squadron at Revel; that, whenever the British and Swedish fleets should arrive, and under protection of a flag of truce send in any letters, they should be met at a considerable distance, and not suffered to come near the works. Then they might be taken, but with this limitation;—no letter directed to the Tsar himself to be received, unless it came immediately from a crowned head. After this adjustment of things the cruisers stationed at proper distances, a good way in sea, upon the appearance of the British and Swedish squadrons on the 30th of May under the command of the Honourable Sir John Norris, and Admiral Count Sparre,[1] firing several guns, the preconcerted signal, retired into their havens, whereupon a general alarm was given by setting fire to the beacons all along the coast. When the combined fleet came to anchor under the island Nargen, a flag of truce was sent off from Revel to Sir John Norris with letters, which were answered by him; and soon after the boats returned a second [time] with a reply.

The Russian fleet thus obstructed from going to sea, the Tsar determined to prove some new ships; and pursuant thereto, in person, attended by the General-Admiral and the two Rear-Admirals Sievers and Gordon, sailed about five leagues distance from Kronslot, and spent some days in trying the Hangö Head, Lesnoy, Fredrikstadt, North Eagle and Isaak Victoria. All answered tolerably well, except the Lesnoy, whose masts were ordered to be reduced a second time.

[1] Count Clas Sparre; b. January 6, 1675, d. April 25, 1732. High Admiral (*Öfver Amiral*) and President (1719) of the Swedish Royal *Amiralitets-Kollegium* (*Biogr. Lexikon*, &c., Stockholm, vol. xv.).

XVII. DIGRESSION CONCERNING GENERAL-ADMIRAL COUNT APRAXIN.

Frederick Count Apraxin,[1] General-Admiral, &c., sprung from the ancient Russian nobility, and related at a distance to the Tsar, is about sixty-four[2] years of age, of a moderate height, well-made, fair, inclining to feed, curious[3] of his hair, [which is] very long and now grey; and generally wears it tied up with a ribbon. A native cleanness adds a lustre to the dignity of his magnificent mien, wherein he surpasses all the noblemen of his years in Russia. Although a widower of a long date, is without issue, yet you observe an incomparable economy, order and decency in his house, gardens, domestics and dress. All that have the honour to be thoroughly acquainted with him, unanimously vote in behalf of his excellent temper; but he loves to have men comport themselves according to their rank, and expects from all that approach him a due and adequate respect; nor dare the Court buffoons, even in the presence of the Tsar, take their usual liberties in Count Apraxin's palace. Sobriety and early rising

---

[1] The first name of this distinguished Russian was Feodore (*Theodore*). Feodore Matveievitz Apraxin was born 1671, and died November 20, 1728. Kleinschmidt (p. 177) says, 'Apraxin was the real creator of the Russian navy.' He was, beyond dispute, Peter's most efficient native fellow-worker in creating a fleet. In 1710 he was given the title of Count. In 1711 he commanded in the Black Sea. His services in the Baltic are recounted in the text. In 1722 he accompanied Peter in his Persian campaign, and was the first to fly an admiral's flag in the Caspian Sea (Kleinschmidt, pp. 177-8).

[2] He was really about 54. The substitution of 64 for the real number is probably due to the copyist of the original MS.

[3] 'Curious. † 1. Bestowing care or pains; careful, studious, attentive' (*New English Dictionary*).

greatly recommend to his notice, and he espouses the interests of his dependents with the care and zeal of a father; but takes none into his protection till he perfectly knows their capacity and manner of living, since if he once professed friendship, will never desert their cause, though sure to incur thereby the Tsar's displeasure. And as he is on many accounts a very valuable friend, so no less dangerous an enemy, ever intent on time and place to effect his resentment. Sincerity is his darling distinguishing virtue; and upon a promise to procure justice, or do a good office to a man, if he perceives in his face a diffidence, arising from the known perfidious usage in such cases universally obtaining in Russia, he will lay his hand on his breast and say, ' I, Apraxin, give you my word.' After this sanction to be received as sacred, he exerts all his powers to perform his engagement; and, if opposed by the Sovereign's absolute will, will yet maintain the justice of the demand till the Tsar, in a passion, by his menaces enforces silence. And then I have known him at his public levée, report the issue to the person aloud in the audience of the whole assembly, saying, 'Friend! I have done all within the verge of my abilities to accomplish your desire; and solemnly assure you it's none of my fault if your petition is not granted.' His constitution inclines to phlegmatic, and consequently [he] is averse to rash precipitate measures; but as General many years of the army,[1] has given undeniable proofs of his courage and illustrious ones of his conduct. From a diametrical opposition in their genius, he is rather esteemed than beloved by the Tsar; and therefore rarely consulted, unless on arduous and important affairs. The Tsar oft visits him, but he seldom appears at

---

[1] He held command of the land forces, as well as of the naval, operating in Finland till the winter of 1719-20 (see p. 87).

Court, except on public days; and is very shy and reserved to the Tsar's creatures. Whoever pays his devoirs to the one is regarded by the other with an eye of jealousy. However, he is thought to be heartily attached to that Prince's interests; though at the same time, in confidence with his intimates, will lament the deplorable condition of his native country, amidst so great a series of success. Notwithstanding the disadvantages of having never seen the world abroad, nor understanding foreign languages, never gone through the rudiments of a seaman, nor ever been at sea till advanced in years, yet by the force of admirable natural parts and a prodigious memory, [he] has attained to a sufficient competency of maritime skill, and supports to amazement the authority of High Admiral held by so precarious a tenure in that arbitrary Government; even when the Tsar, as inferior flag officer, differing in notion, will endeavour to invalidate the General-Admiral's opinion, by alleging his inexperience as having never seen foreign navies, Count Apraxin will instantly retort the same invidious charge, to the utmost provocation of the Tsar; though afterwards will submit with the following alleviation: 'Whilst I as admiral argue with your Majesty in quality of flag officer, I can never give way; but if you assume the Tsar, I know my duty.' And if the Tsar without acquainting him, prefers a man out of caprice without any distinguishing merit, he postpones both commission and pay till the usual time of advancement, New Year's Day, or at least till he has made a more regular application. He is the youngest of three brothers, all now, or lately, living, of the name of Apraxin, and the only one of the ancient Russ nobility that in every critical exigency may indisputably be styled the oracle and *dernier ressort*[1]

[1] MS. 'Dernier's resort.'

of the imperial administration. This is his just character, and the result of my personal observation, though I am sensible a different account has been given in some less momentous points; and, peradventure, in some few instances, when his spirit has been exhausted by an intense application to a multiplicity of weighty affairs, and his temper ruffled by an importunate address, he may have received some persons with incomplaisance; and he has been taxed with a misapplication of public moneys, the epidemical vice of the Russian nation.

[*Here the Digression ends.*]

From thence the Tsar went to Viborg, and the ships into haven. The three Russ snows commanded by Captain Villebois and Captain-Lieutenants Apraxin and Lopakin that wintered at Danzig, being obliged to depart, in consequence of a capitulation betwixt that city and the commander of a Swedish squadron, wherein likewise the Swedes were restrained from pursuing them, made the best of their way to Riga, to avoid the British and Swedish fleets then lying before Revel.

XVIII. PROCEEDINGS IN 1721.

The greatest part of the galleys, wintering at Åbö, Helsingfors and Viborg, rendezvous'd in the spring under General Galitzin, commander of the army in Finland for some years past; though till this season the General-Admiral Apraxin had the supreme direction in carrying on the conquests on that side; and would by no means suffer this general, a bold daring man, to undertake anything of moment. But now he readily consented to his commanding in chief, for Count Apraxin, a gentleman of much humanity and compassion, virtues rarely found in the native Russ, willingly declined acting a second part of the barbarous ravages of the foregoing year. The proceedings of the galleys and the havoc and ruin[1] accomplished in Sweden were written in too legible characters and are too recent in the memory of mankind to need a repetition.

Some Swedish frigates, cruising at the entrance of the Norr Botten,[2] to prevent, if possible, the crossing over of the Russ galleys from the Finnish to the Swedish shore, observed here and there a straggling galley lying amongst the islands[3] and rocks wherewith that coast abounds; and imprudently venturing in to attack them in that situation were no sooner entered than the rest of the galleys that lay concealed at a little distance, moving to their companions' assistance, surrounded the Swedes on every side. The largest frigate, touching upon a rock, was boarded and taken; and two others shared in the same misfortune, being swallowed up with numbers that swarmed in upon them from every quarter: the fourth not got so far in among the rocks, retreating, escaped. These frigates of about thirty, twenty-four and eighteen guns were carried with their people to St. Petersburg, where great rejoicings were made and the officers and men led in a public procession of triumph.

[1] See p. 69, note 1.
[2] MS. 'North Bottom.'
[3] The expression 'islands and rocks' is a translation of the Swedish word *skärgård* (pronounced sharegord). A chart of Finland or of Sweden north of Kalmar Sound shows how thickly studded the coast is with islets and rocks. Mankell begins his history (*Studier öfver Svenska Skärgårds-Flottans Historia*, Stockholm, 1855) with an allusion to the 'peculiar natural formation called skärgård.'

A List of the Ships in a condition to go to Sea this Year.

Ships	Guns	Ships	Guns
Hangö Head	90	Britannia	52
Lesnoy	90	Randolph	52
Fredrikstadt	90	Pearl	52
North Eagle	80	Egudel	52
Marlborough	70	Ormonde	52
Neptunus	70	Varakiel	52
St. Alexander	70	Uriel	52
Isaak Victoria	64	L'Espérance	44
Moscow	64	Arundel	48
Ingermanland	64	Wachtmeister	44
Slutelburg	64	Raphael	40
Revel	64	Samson	32
Devonshire	60	*pink*, Alexander	24
Katharina	60	New Kronslot	16

Several ships more this year were condemned as unfit for service; and the latter end of this summer the fortifications on the avenues of Kronslot were finished; and now this place was first accounted impregnable. In the winter more advancements [were] made among the officers of the fleet than any one year before; but they generally fell to the share of the Russ. The Admiralty College having contracted for a considerable quantity of Spanish salt, the same was imported and applied to the seasoning of the parts [1] observed to be so soon decayed last year. This was the Tsar's expedient, upon a supposal that a proper application of salt would harden the timber and plank, and prevent the mouldy dampness engendered by the fresh water and hard frosts.

Captain van Werden arrived from Astrakhan, whither he had been sent in 1717 with several other officers, to make discoveries on the Caspian Sea, so little known to Europe. He perfected an accurate chart, the best now extant, of the rivers, roads, and harbours; and it is conjectured this con-

---

[1] Of the ships. See *ante*, p. 73.

tributed not a little to induce the Tsar to undertake his late expedition.

The great project of peace rendered the preparations less this spring, 1721, than usual. However, half the ships were careened ; and this method is annually observed whereby every ship, once in two years, comes under a thorough inspection. Several new officers, principally Danes, arrived. The Tsar having three ships in Holland, built for his use some time ago, now deemed it a convenient season to bring them round ; and accordingly despatched Captains Zachary Mishecoff, James Laurence, and Jacob Savage, with their proper officers and a good number of men in the Egudel and Uriel for that purpose. Three new ships were likewise launched and named, the St. Katharina, Freedmaker and Astrakhan : the old Katharina assuming the name of Viborg.

The Kronslot squadron went out some five or six leagues and continued awhile in exercising and forming lines of battle. Several captains not observing their proper stations, incurred the Tsar's displeasure ; and being taken in arrest were confined and ordered to be mulcted of part of their pay ; but the news of the peace [1] supervening, they shared in the benefit of the general amnesty. Much about this time arrived at St. Petersburg Vice-Admiral Wilster, with his two sons, from Sweden ; the motives of quitting his former employment, and addressing himself to the Tsar, are remote from this design. In the beginning of the late war, he was a rear-admiral in the Danish service ; but upon an affair, differently related, declared incapable of

---

[1] The treaty of Nystädt (or Neustadt) was signed on $\frac{\text{August } 30}{\text{September } 10}$, 1721. It is given entire, as a supplement to his *Histoire de Russie sous Pierre le Grand*, by Voltaire (*Œuvres Complètes*, Paris, 1878, xvi. p. 630).

serving any longer in Denmark. Obtaining leave to go abroad, he went to Sweden, was there accepted, and signalised himself in an action against the Danes. He was well received and caressed by the Tsar; and sits constantly in the College as Vice-Admiral. One of his sons [was] made a captain, and the other a captain-lieutenant.

XIX. DIGRESSION ON THE RELATIONS BETWEEN ADMIRALS GORDON AND SIEVERS.[1]

Several signal victories are annually commemorated with much pomp and ceremony, and the commandant of any place of distinction has a proper allowance for these public entertainments. Whilst they [the ships] were now out came on the celebration of the anniversary[2] of the Battle of Hangö Head, in 1714, wherein, as before related, the Swedish Rear-Admiral Ehrenskiöld was taken prisoner: the Prince on this occasion not having his flag hoisted is to be considered as Tsar.

At this entertainment, when the whole company was inflamed with wine, always plentiful on these solemnities, Rear-Admiral Gordon represented to the Tsar in the Hollands language, several things to the disadvantage of Rear-Admiral Sievers, and particularly that he did not show him the respect due to his character, in not consulting with him on affairs of moment, nor communicating the orders he received from the College[3] any otherways than to the captains. And farther, as the College only appointed the captains their respective ships,

---

[1] This digression is written in a contemporary hand, but one different from that of the rest of the MS. It covers both pages of a leaf which seems to have been inserted amongst the others when the MS. was bound.
[2] July 27, 1714. See p. 37.   [3] The Admiralty.

leaving the distribution of lieutenants and all inferiors to Sievers, he had taken the advantage of his power to assign the best officers and men to the Danish and Dutch commanders; whilst he and the rest of his party being Britons were so wretchedly provided, that should they be ordered out to sea they were utterly unable to manage their ships and must infallibly suffer in their reputation; at the same time his Majesty running the utmost risk of losing his men of war; and so artfully couching his discourse, as to insinuate they were persecuted for their principles even in Russia.

The General-Admiral in vain endeavoured to interrupt the discourse, or persuade the Tsar to remove from Gordon and sit by him. He would hear all the Rear-Admiral had to say, and then began to expostulate in high terms with the General-Admiral, ever using this expression in an upbraiding manner, 'You and your Rear-Admiral do this and that'; threatening them with the loss of their heads if any damage was sustained by their maladministration.

The General-Admiral laboured all in his power to justify Sievers, and when occasion led him to mention Gordon, retorted upon the Tsar, 'Your Rear-Admiral.' Sievers, thoroughly acquainted with the Russian freedom in liquor, took no notice, but left the company. Gordon, totally ignorant of the Russian language, and none presuming to interpret what the General-Admiral said of him, was silent. Nevertheless, the dispute was carried very high betwixt the Tsar and the General-Admiral; Count Apraxin declaring that he looked upon Gordon and his associates as men of turbulent dispositions and malevolent principles; that having set their native country in a flame[1] without finding their account in

[1] This suggests that some of the British officers who took service with Peter were refugee Jacobites.

it some of them were forced to fly from justice, and were now caballing to foment divisions in Russia. However, in conclusion, the Tsar obliged the General-Admiral to submit, and the assembly broke up.

In the morning the Tsar, reflecting on what had passed, waited upon the General-Admiral and according to the Russian custom said, 'My lord, I was drunk[1] last night. Excuse anything said or done amiss.' The Admiral replied, 'As for me, I am your Majesty's subject and slave, and your Majesty may do what you please with me for speaking my sentiments without reserve; but Sievers is no Russian, neither will he put up [with] such indignities, after so many years' faithful service. Your Majesty must be sensible how much we owe to him for our fleet's arrival in its present formidable height, nor do I know a man in your Majesty's dominions equally qualified to do you future service in your maritime affairs. For my part I do not pretend to it; and why Gordon, perfectly unacquainted with the Russian language and customs, should be more in your Majesty's good graces than he, I profess I am perfectly at a loss to account for. I expect Sievers will demand his dismission at the end of the campaign; and if he goes, many will be ready for the flag; but I know of none capacitated to go through the multiplicity of business in his arduous employment.' The Tsar said little in vindication; only that Gordon was a brave officer, and had served long in a better regulated navy than ever Sievers did.

[1] Peter made this excuse more than once. 'En mai 1703 je trouve sous sa plume, dans un billet adressé à Féodor Apraxine, ces lignes significatives : " Comment je vous ai quitté je ne saurais le dire, car j'étais trop comblé par les présents de Bacchus. Aussi je vous demande à tous de me pardonner si j'ai pu faire de la peine à quelques-uns d'entre vous . . . et d'oublier ce qui s'est passé "' (Waliszewski, *Pierre le Grand*, Paris, 1897, p. 130).

The Tsar then asked Sievers to excuse what was past, and desired him to live in amity with Gordon as his brother rear-admiral, and thereby ease himself of part of the burden or weight of affairs that lay upon him. But Sievers maintained that Gordon had falsely accused him of partiality in dividing the officers and men; that consulting him would sooner embarrass than ease him in the province under his care; and that whilst he served his Majesty, was Gordon's senior officer and superior flag, his Majesty must excuse his non-admission of him upon the proposed foot of equality; but as soon as the campaign was over, his Majesty might redress all grievances by granting him the dismission he had long desired, and should insist upon; and then his Majesty might do his pleasure in giving Mr. Gordon the flag, and the affairs under his direction.

The Tsar, with some difficulty, got 'em to drink a glass together, under the mask of a seeming reconciliation; but as their variance had been of an old date, and diffused itself amongst the officers, most of them espousing one side or the other, the emulation survives; Sievers still retaining, and using with a high hand, his power; and has gained over to his party Rear-Admiral Saunders.

A List of the Tsar's Fleet capable of going to Sea, though many of them not equipped this Year.[1]

Ships	Guns	Commanders
Hangö Head	90	Hoogstraten
Lesnoy	90	Ivan Sinavin
Fredrikstadt	90	Falkenberg
North Eagle	80	Armitage
Marlborough	70	Bering
St. Alexander	70	Brant
Neptunus	70	Tressel

[1] This list and that given at p. 82 refer to 1721, the year of the peace.

Ships	Guns	Commanders
Katharina	70	Smith
Freedmaker	90	Van Werden
Isaak Victoria	64	Antufiof
Astrakhan	64	Gosler
Moscow	64	Hay
Ingermanland	64	Bredale
Revel	64	Van Werden
Slutelburg	64	Wessel
Devonshire	60	Zotoff
Viborg	60	Bents
Britannia	52	Chapezan
Randolph	52	Masnoy
Pearl	52	Kasheloff
Egudel	52	Laurence
Varakiel	52	Van Rosen
Uriel	52	Turnhoud
Ormonde	52	Delap
Arundel	48	Muconoff
L'Esperance	44	Knee
Wachtmeister	44	Carabin
Raphael	40	Lenoy
Amsterdam Galley	36	Golovin

Several others of smaller force.

Peace being proclaimed in September, several promotions ensued, without staying for New Year's Day, the usual period of preferment.

Vice-Admiral Cruys	Admiral of the Blue
Vice-Admiral Peter Alexeievitz (the Tsar)	Admiral of the Red
Prince Alexander Menshikoff	Vice-Admiral of the White
Rear-Admiral Sievers	Vice-Admiral of the Blue
Rear-Admiral Gordon	Vice-Admiral of the Red
Rear-Admiral Imaivitz of the Galleys	Vice-Admiral of the same
Captain-Commodore Saunders	Rear-Admiral of the White
Captain-Commodore Nahum Sinavin	Rear-Admiral of the Blue
Captain-Commodore Van Hofft	Rear-Admiral of the Red
Captains Bredale, Gosler, and Ivan Sinavin	Captains-Commodores

Van Hofft, raised to rear-admiral, is a Brabanter, an old experienced seaman, but suffers himself to be imposed upon by the intrigues of the Russians. He brought the engine for spouting liquid fire in esteem with the Tsar. Several Russians of inferior rank were also advanced; and Commodore Bredale sent to notify the peace in Holland, France, and Spain. It's thought the Tsar looks upon foreigners promoted at this crisis of time as obliged in point of gratitude to serve during life. One of the new ships of 54 guns, coming from Holland, was cast away near the Island Ösel; Captain Mishecoff, the commander, being a favourite of the Tsar's, little notice was taken of it. Captain Little and the mate sentenced two years ago were now restored; and several other officers under the Tsar's displeasure pardoned and recalled out of exile. Two new ships were launched, called the St. Peter and St. Andrea, and his best ships salted as in the preceding year.

XX. ARRANGEMENTS FOR 1722.

The Tsar, travelling in the winter to Moscow, took in his retinue Vice-Admiral Sievers and Rear-Admiral Saunders; and now resolving upon his Persian expedition, timber was prepared at Kazan for carriages of 200 large cannon; and about 300 miles beyond Moscow, on the Volga, 200 vessels built for transporting the army. All sorts of equipage, and other necessaries, not to be provided in that part of the country, were sent from St. Petersburg; as also Captain-Commodore Gosler, Captains Villebois, Van Werden, Colmeroff, Golovin, Carabin, and Masnoy, with a considerable number of lieutenants, surgeons, under-officers and seamen; the Russian officers in general choosing to serve on the Caspian Sea rather than continue on the Baltic. In February Vice-Admiral Sievers and

Rear-Admiral Saunders returned to St. Petersburg; and some days after Vice-Admiral Gordon and Captain Lane set out for Moscow. Lane was advanced to the character of captain-commodore and salary of rear-admiral. This man projected the model and carried on the works of the haven, and fortifications of Kronslot; as since likewise those of the dock and basin there: and having, by the Tsar's appointment, this winter surveyed Råger Wik, where great preparations were making to form a commodious haven; the Tsar, approving of the plan now by him presented, ordered him to have the superintendency over the works.

The Tsar determining to conduct in person,[1] with the General-Admiral, the approaching enterprise; and yet desirous in the meanwhile to cultivate discipline in his seamen on the Baltic; gave orders for a squadron to go out under the command of Vice-Admiral Gordon; of whose capacity that way he conceived a good opinion from his long serving in the British, justly esteemed by the Tsar the best regulated navy in the world. Designing also to amuse the Danes, he directed the refitting of near 100 galleys. This likewise concurred to give Vice-Admiral Gordon the preference in point of command before Vice-Admiral Sievers, a Dane by birth and appointed to sit in the College this summer. These movements created in many a belief of something extraordinary intended on this, as well [as] on the other side of his dominions; but nothing of moment occurred on the Baltic; only Vice-Admiral Gordon, with about fourteen sail of the ships of the line, departing five or six leagues from Kronslot, continued out near three months; sometimes under sail disciplining the people in forming lines of battle, other whiles at anchor, exercising their guns, and

[1] See *post*, p. 122, note 1.

practising all the different parts of the duty of a seaman. The squadron at Revel, under the command of Rear-Admiral Van Hofft, went through the same naval discipline. Two ships of 54 guns each, Captains Laurence and Savage, arrived this spring from Holland; the Egudel, infirm and unfit for service, being sold there.

A List of the Ships in a capacity of going to Sea, though many of them not equipped this Year.[1]

Ships	Guns
Hangö Head	90
Lesnoy	90
Fredrikstadt	90
St. Peter	90
St. Andrea	90
North Eagle (Severnoi Oril)	80
Neptunus	70
Katharina	70
Freedmaker	90
St. Alexander	70
Marlborough	70
Pantaloon Victoria	70
Isaak Victoria	64
Astrakhan	64
Moscow	64
Ingermanland	64
Revel	64
Slutelburg	64
Viborg	60
Devonshire	60
Poltava	56
Prince Eugene	54
Crown de Lieft	36
Britannia	52
Randolph	52
Ormonde	52
Pearl	52
Arundel	48
L'Espérance	44
Wachtmeister	44
Amsterdam Galley	36
Samson (*rebuilt*)	32

Several of less force.

[1] A.D. 1722.

The principal captains remaining at Kronslot and Revel were Hoogstraten, Falkenberg, Armitage, Bering, Brant, Bents, Chapezan, Zotoff, Van Rosen, Delap, Muconoff, Hay, Little, Wilster, Stubbs, Antufiof, Kasheloff.

Lord Duffus, arriving this summer at St. Petersburg, was, by the first report, to be superintendent of the yard, where the ships are built, and naval magazines kept, with a salary of 1,000 roubles per annum;[1] this charge, in part, agreeing with a commissioner's of one of his Majesty's yards in Great Britain.

Several storeships of the greatest burden were employed this summer in transporting large timber from Finland, for the use of the haven they intended to begin this winter at Råger Wik, it being the properest season for works of this kind, when all is fast frozen over. Great numbers of people were also assembled, to get stones together to be applied to this work; and barracks built for their accommodation in the extremity of the cold weather. Yet notwithstanding these great preparations, little was done this winter towards forming the harbour; many coincidents contributing to retard, at least for a time, its accomplishment. For the undertakers of the canal of communication betwixt the Volkov and Neva, to avoid some hills in the way, conducting their channel all along the low ground in a semicircle of a great extent, were at last unable to carry on their works through a large morass; and the Tsar, understanding this, at his return from Persia ordered away Captain-Commodore Lane, before appointed

---

[1] The salary of a commissioner in an English dockyard was 500*l.*, late in the seventeenth and early in the eighteenth centuries (*British Archæological Association*, February 2, 1898; *Notes on a MS. of Edward Battine*, by I. Chalkley Gould, pp. 236, 245, 248). See *post*, p. 100, note 1.

to direct the works of Råger Wik, now to survey the canal performance and the situation of the country. He is a sober ingenious man and has done great things for the Tsar. Finding, upon a thorough inspection, the present course impracticable, he advised to desist there, and attempt the prosecution of this project another way; whereby the achievement of two or three years' labour was rendered in the main insignificant and useless.

Another obstruction is the many great works that Prince had in hand in this part of his dominions contiguous to the Baltic; and again, though Russia abounds in grain, annually exporting great quantities, yet this year it suffered under a scarcity of bread corn, partly occasioned by an indifferent crop, but principally [by] draining the country of its ordinary supplies to support the Caspian expedition. Add to these, peradventure, the main impediments, absence of money and aversion of the Russian populace to works of this nature, proceeding from an universal distaste and dissatisfaction, prevailing in the body of the Russian nation, for reasons easily assignable but reserved to a proper opportunity. However, the Russ give them in a summary comprehensive proverb: *Do Bogha visoko, do Tsaria daleko.* 'God is far above us—and the Tsar far from us.'

Besides the ships of war, frigates, snows, *prahms*, bomb-ketches, and brigantines, the Tsar has a considerable number of vessels, from 50 to 500 tons,[1] fit either for transports or storeships; near fifty whereof were taken in 1718 and 1719 from all nations trading to the Baltic; but Lübeck and Danzig were the greatest sufferers: the rest were chiefly built of fir timber, on the Ladoga Lake.

[1] MS. 'tun.'

XXI. AN ACCOUNT OF THE GALLEY FLEET.

It may not seem eccentric to this design to say something of the vessels so frequently mentioned under the denomination of galleys.[1] Their builders were generally Italian, as also their sea officers, intermingled with Greeks. Nor is the Tsar ambitious that a Russian should enjoy that title; only, he desires that his military officers, with their respective companies, should so far understand their discipline as to command and manage these vessels upon occasion. Of the nations above mentioned the Tsar has one vice-admiral, two captain-commodores, about twenty captains, and about as many lieutenants, with forty under-officers, such as boatswains and boatswains' mates. The officers of the men-of-war seldom care to converse much with these people; partly on account of their different languages and manner of living; but more out of abhorrence of the great barbarities they have sometimes practised upon an enemy, when in their power; nor are the latter allowed to rank with them upon a foot of equality. Notwithstanding this general character, the present Vice-Admiral Ismaivitz is a man of generosity, and a good soldier. It is the duty of these officers, with soldiers appointed to assist them, to see the galleys equipped and duly

[1] The regular fleet and the galley fleet were distinct organisations in several countries—for example, Russia, France, and Sweden. It is evident from the tone of the remarks in the text that the officers of the navy proper looked down upon, 'seldom cared to converse much with,' those of the galley fleet, who were considered members of a distinct and inferior service. It has been seen that the Russian victory of Hangö Head was not won by the Russian navy, but by the galleys. (For the French galley fleet see Père Daniel, *Histoire de la Milice Française*; for the Swedish, see the works of Bäckström and Mankell cited on former pages.) Also see Appendix C.

provided with necessaries for sea against the army embarks. For ten years past the Tsar has left off building, what may properly be called 'half-galleys,' as approving more of *scampavias*,[1] vessels of the same form exactly, but much less and rowing better. Besides six or eight half-galleys, dignified with proper names, and reserved to accommodate the Tsar, General-Admiral, Vice-Admiral Ismaivitz, and other eminent persons, the rest are distinguished by the following method. Each general has such a number assigned, in proportion to the men under his command, as answers to about 200 men per vessel. On the stern of the General's galley, or *scampavia*, is No. 1, and so on successive numbers in the stern of every vessel, to the extent of his division. These divisions are known apart by their proper colours, white, blue, red, and farther, if necessity require, by a regular variation their sub-divisions also. The sea officers appertaining to these galleys are distributed amongst them, as far as they will go: and any deficiency supplied out of the Russ under-officers and sailors. The Tsar has about 200 of this sort of vessels; and can, it is supposed, in three months' time build 50 more upon any emergency. Besides these, he had a considerable number of large *lotkeys*, much resembling *scampavias*, but still less, computed at 70 or 80 men each, of late years accompanying the others in all their expeditions on the coast of Finland and Sweden. In these vessels that never come in any great sea, nor the men obliged to go aloft, the Russians are very handy; as likewise, in building these *lotkeys*, performed by the soldiers without a master's direction, and seldom with any other tool but a hatchet; in management whereof they certainly exceed all nations under the sun. All other tools

[1] MS. 'scampafie.'

are of late date amongst them, and still by many accounted foreign ; up in the country none to be found, for as they have plenty of wood they want no saw to make boards, but splitting[1] the timber, hew it to a convenient proportion, never making more than two planks of the thickness of a tree.

XXII. PAY OF OFFICERS AND DOCKYARD OFFICIALS.

Vice-Admiral Cruys is highly blamed by all foreign officers in the Tsar's service, he being the only man that might have influenced him to allow good pay at the commencement of the establishment; at least, that some equitable proportion should have been observed between the different appointments.[2]

---

[1] In Tasmania, and also in some parts of Australia, 'splitting' is in common use. Trunks of the hardwood (*Eucalyptus*) trees are split into short narrow planks with a single tool, and the amount of work done by one man in a working-day is astonishing to a stranger.

[2] As the foreign officers who entered the Russian service under Peter the Great were not all—as some few of those of British nationality were—driven from their own country by political troubles, it might be presumed that the rates of pay in Russia were designedly made sufficient to attract them. This, however, does not appear to have been the case. A comparison between the rates of pay in the British and in the Russian navies in the earlier years of the eighteenth century shows that the former—even when the exchange value of the rouble was at its highest—was more liberal than the latter. When the rouble in exchange fell to 50 per cent. of its former value, the Russian rate compares very unfavourably with the British.

In Russia, with the rouble = 10*s*., the highest captain's pay was 20*l*. a month ; in the British Navy it was 21*l*. The Russian captain was allowed at first 'six common peasants,' afterwards reduced to three. The British captain was allowed at first about thirty servants, and in 1705, eight. Assuming that in each case the captain—either by taking it, or by saving an equivalent expense for wages—counted the pay of these men amongst his allowances,

UNDER PETER THE GREAT

		Roubles
Vice-Admiral Cruys, 3 per cent. out of all prizes and a salary per annum		3,000
Vice-Admirals	from 16 to	1,800
Rear-Admiral		100
Captain-Commodore		50
First Rank Captain		40
Second Rank Captain		30
Third Rank Captain	According to the	25
Captain Lieutenant	common Russian	20
First Lieutenant	establishment per	15
Second Lieutenant	month	10
Surgeons	from 10 to	15
Steersman or Mate	from 10 to	15
Boatswain and Gunner		10
Boatswain's Mate		7
Foreign Seamen		5

Commission officers, Russian born, have the same pay with foreigners; only the Russians have the additional income to the Russian would have been, first, 9*l.* (18 roubles), and then 4*l.* 10*s.* (9 roubles) a month; whilst the British captain's monthly income in connexion with servants was calculated at 36*l.* 6*s.* When the latter's servants were reduced in number to eight, his pay was increased to 42*l.* Thus, whilst the total monthly emolument of the senior captains in the Russian Navy was before the fall of the rouble 29*l.*, captains of British first rates received 54*l.* 6*s.*, and, when the rate of pay was reduced in 1705, 49*l.* 4*s.*

The highest pay of a Russian lieutenant was—rouble = 10*s.*— 7*l.* 10*s.* a month; the lowest 5*l.* The highest pay of a British lieutenant was 8*l.* 8*s.*, and the lowest 7*l.*

In other ranks the Russian pay—as long as the rouble would exchange for 10*s.*—was higher than the British. In the Russian service, surgeons received from 7*l.* to 5*l.* a month; in the British service, the uniform monthly remuneration of surgeons was 5*l.* Gunners and boatswains in the Russian Navy received 5*l.* a month; in the British from 4*l.* to 2*l.* 10*s.* When the rouble fell to 5*s.* exchange value, 2*l.* 10*s.* was the Russian uniform rate. Foreign seamen in Russia received 2*l.* 10*s.* a month, against the 1*l.* 4*s.* of a British A.B. When the rouble was at its lowest, the difference between the two rates was only 1*s.*

The pay of British naval officers was relatively much higher at the beginning of the last century than it is at the close of this. For the higher ranks it was not much lower, absolutely, than the

H

but twelve, whereas foreigners are allowed thirteen, months to the year.

		Roubles
Russian Boatswain	⎫	7
Boatswain's Mate	⎬ per month	5
Russian seaman that has served abroad; of which there are but few	⎭	3

Other sailors divided into	first rank . per month	1	⎫
	second rank ,,	70	⎬ kopieiki
	third rank . ,,	40	⎭
Cabin boys .	. . . ,,	30	

100 kopieiki make a rouble. Besides this pay the sailors have a constant allowance of coarse clothing, and a provision of rye-meal, oatmeal, and salt; even when the sea service is over.

Notwithstanding, this general rule admits of particular exceptions; as in the case of Rear-Admiral Paddon, Vice-Admiral Gordon, and Rear-Admiral Saunders, besides their established pay from the College of Admiralty annually receiving out of the

---

present. Professor Laughton (*Journal of the Royal United Service Institution*, June 25, 1880) gives the pay of a captain of a first rate in 1690 as 763*l.* 15*s.* This was in a generation in which, as Macaulay tells us, the average income of a baronet was estimated 'at 900*l.* a year, the average income of a member of the House of Commons at less than 800*l.* a year. A thousand a year was thought a large revenue for a barrister.'

As compared with the wages of able seamen—24*s.* with board and lodging for twenty-eight days—we may quote Thorold Rogers (*Hist. of Agriculture and Prices*, 1887, vol. v. p. 404): 'Up to the end of the second quarter of the eighteenth century, the wages of the artisan were 1*s.* 6*d.* to 2*s.* a day,' without board or lodging. In 1767 a labourer's board and washing were estimated as amounting in money to about 12*l.* a year—that is 20*s.* a month.

This history makes it clear that the amount of legitimate prize-money to be gained by the officers of the Russian fleet in general was not large. Plunder fell exclusively to the share of the officers of the galley fleet, in which British officers did not serve. For comparison between Russian and English rates of pay see Appendix E.

Tsar's cabinet, or privy purse, certain sums under the appellation of a free gift, or bounty money, to exclude all pretensions of others.

About twenty years ago [1] a rouble, according to the course of exchange, was rated at about ten shillings ; whereas at present it yields no more than five shillings, the intrinsic value being equally reduced by a great alloy in the coin.[2] Besides this loss the foreign officers have been abridged in the number of their servants ; formerly a captain was allowed six common peasants given by the Tsar, and by him paid and victualled ; but before the peace they were reduced to three, and the captain-lieutenants and lieutenants in proportion. Every officer advanced is obliged to give one month's pay to the hospital ; and since the peace, 25 kopieiki per rouble, or 25 per cent., deducted from the pay of those that have been at any time preferred ; as also, the thirteenth month is taken away from foreigners, though continuing in the same station. Formerly they were usually paid four months in advance, at farthest, as soon as it was due ; but now they are near a year in arrears. These deductions and defalcations have reduced them to very mean circumstances.

[1] In 1704.
[2] The fall in the value of the rouble was due partly to variation in the exchange and partly to an alteration of the coinage. The following account is taken from the fifth edition of Meyer's *Konversations-Lexikon* (1896), vol. xiv. p. 974. *Roubles*, as pieces cut from silver bars (*Griwenka*), were first mentioned in 1321. About 1665 silver and copper roubles, with the arms of Moskow, were coined, but the latter only for a short time. From 1704 Peter the Great had coined the rouble (*moneta dobraja*, good money). $\frac{31}{34}$ fine = 4·3735 marks ; gold to silver being $15\frac{1}{2}$ to 1. From 1711 the rouble was coined as *moneta novaja* (new money), $\frac{34}{44}$ fine = 3·7325 marks. According to Zedler's *Universal Lexikon*, vol. xxxii. (1742), p. 1399, the rouble was then worth 30 to 32 'good groschen.'

The Shipbuilders' Pay.[1]

	Roubles.
Cosens, Ney, and Brown have each per ann. abt.	1,000
And Brown over and above, in consideration of his directing the repairing of the fleet at Kronslot . . . . . per month	40
Ramsey at St. Petersburg, and Davenport at Revel with the charge of repairs there, each per annum	800
Hadley at Kazan, on account of cheapness of provisions . . . . per annum	600
Builders' Assistants . . . per month	84

Cosens, Ney, and Brown, at the time of their engaging in the Tsar's service, contracted for the payment of the greatest part of their salary in England; but since for some reasons departing from that agreement receive it in Russia, and have some allowance on account of the diminution of the value of the coins above related.

This disproportion betwixt the salary of a master builder, and the pay of a captain in the navy, has been a source of continual discontent. In 1720 the Tsar established the point of precedency, when the master builders were assigned the degree of third rank captains; wherein they held themselves as much aggrieved as the captains in the article of pay.

Besides the English shipbuilders, the Tsar has

---

[1] Differing from those ruling in the navy the rates of pay for dockyard officials in Russia in Peter the Great's time were higher than in England. When Sir Phineas Pett, in April, 1696, was appointed Resident Commissioner for Chatham and Sheerness, his salary was fixed at 500*l.* a year. He had one clerk with 50*l.* a year, and one with 30*l.* (J. R. Tanner, *English Historical Review*, January 1899, p. 67). Mr. Brown at Kronslot had 1,000 roubles a year, and 40 r. for thirteen months; in all, 1,520 r., which, when the salary was established, equalled 760*l.* Brown's position was a lower one than that of Sir Phineas Pett, and the former and his associates were, as stated in the text, indemnified—at least to some extent—for the fall in the exchange value of the rouble.

three of his own subjects, that have built several ships; their names, Fedorsee Sklave, Gabriel Ofdyth, and Philip Palsecoff. To give the Russians the better insight, it is usual when an English master begins a ship, to order a Russian master to set up one of the same dimensions, near at hand; and the Russian must be indulged the liberty of observing and measuring the Englishman's work.

The Tsar always showed great respect to his shipbuilders; frequently on public occasions sitting amongst them and calling himself one of their fraternity. But of late he seldom does them this honour, and this summer has given them much distaste by introducing a custom, that every master builder shall watch his work night and day in the yard at St. Petersburg; to take an exact account of all demands and proceedings in the building of his ships, under pretence of easing the Surveyor-General Golovin, formerly a general in the army. This innovation was strenuously opposed by the shipbuilders, till the Tsar in person confirming it to be his will, required an implicit obedience.

The pay of the foreign officers in the land service is much inferior to those at sea; except in the artillery branch; and the Russians and 'Old Dutch,' to wit, persons born of foreign parents in his dominions, have a very small allowance in regard to their inexperience in the arts of other nations. Very few foreigners in his service, either by land or sea, have been able to make any considerable advantage; and of those few, rarely one permitted to depart the country. Besides long attendance and great expense to procure dismission, various stratagems are used to impoverish 'em in their fortunes. No one maxim obtains more generally than this; and now, if I am not misinformed, prevails more than ever from the highest to the lowest degree.

XXIII. WARRANT OFFICERS AND SEAMEN.

It is very difficult for the Tsar to have any good under officers, or, as they are termed in England, warrant officers, in the Russian navy; because of the very ill usage they meet with from the lieutenants, generally Russians and men of little worth, upon the least provocation; nor are they protected from their barbarous treatment by the Articles of War, or particular instructions given to commission officers.

Nor has he any great opportunities for forming seamen; though the indulgence granted the Tsar, in permitting a considerable number of his young noblemen, gentlemen, and common people, to serve in quality of volunteers in the British and Dutch navies, during the late war with France, contributed something towards supplying him with men of experience of his own nation, but in no degree answerable to his expectations. For the Russians in general have an aversion to sea, and no manner of inspection was made into the genius and inclinations of these youths; many of them sons of such as were suspected to be the least favourable to the Tsar's designs of altering their customs, and new modelling their country; and these retaining a spice of their fathers' disaffection were the less intent on making a progress; and the rest of the men of fashion, having credit at large, launched out into all manner of effeminate and extravagant living, frequenting the play-houses, gaming tables, &c., according to the prevailing gust of the nation they conversed in, not caring how little they went to sea; and upon their recall, undergoing a strict examination, were found instead of attaining the rudiments of a seaman, to have acquired only the insignificant accomplishments of fine gentlemen. And the Tsar, incensed thereat, gave directions to reduce 'em to common seamen, and employed them constantly in the most servile part of their work. In a word, this great expense was to very little purpose; for out of the many sent abroad, there were but few exceptions to this character;[1] only those of meaner circumstances being obliged to be more at sea, of consequence made a better improvement.

It being about twenty years since the Tsar began to build and rig his ships, he has a sufficient number of people tolerably skilled in fixing the rigging and going through all parts of a seaman's duty to be done ashore, or whilst the ship is in the haven, and yet are good for little at sea; and the great want he is in of able seamen outweighs all other difficulties

[1] This contemporary estimate of the result of Peter's efforts to educate a staff of officers for his fleet bears out that formed by Schuyler, whose book was published in 1884. 'Peter sent abroad fifty nobles, representatives of the highest and most distinguished families in the Empire. Twenty-eight were ordered to Italy, especially to Venice, where they might learn the art of building galleys; the remainder to Holland and England. Each was accompanied by a soldier. According to their instructions they were to make themselves familiar with the use of charts, compasses, and navigation; they were to learn thoroughly the art of ship-building, and were to become practised in the duties of common sailors. No one was to return without permission and without a certificate attesting his proficiency, on penalty of confiscation of all his property. They were obliged to pay their own expenses. . . . In point of fact several of them turned their stay abroad to profit, and, like Kurúkin, Dolgorúky, Tolstói, and Hilkof, became skilful diplomatists, able administrators, and useful servants of Peter and his successors; but not one distinguished himself in naval matters' (*Peter the Great*, vol. i. p. 325).

'The navy lacked educated officers, and, in its general decline after Peter's death, even those who could be of service found it better to seek a career in another direction' (*Ibid.*, vol. ii. p. 506).

'En résumé, soit au point de vue militaire, soit au point de vue commerciale, Pierre s'est employé avec autant de passion que d'inutilité à convertir les Russes en un peuple de marins' (Waliszewski, *Pierre le Grand*, Paris, 1897, p. 558).

he has to grapple with; the long winters proving a main impediment to his people's learning that art; since in so long an interval they easily forgot what they but imperfectly knew the foregoing summer. Nay, if a man of some experience comes, and continues a while in their fleet, he must use some address to retain his former acquisitions of knowledge; for as there is neither ebb nor flood in the Baltic, some essentials in a seaman's duty are not to be learned by the ignorant, and persons of some skill in navigation preserve with difficulty the experience they had formerly gained. These, with other reasons, will necessitate the Tsar to be at the constant charge of fitting out annually a squadron of ships of war for sea, be it only to discipline his men.

Boys in the service are of late standing; and the practice of breaking regiments for some years past, and forcing the men to serve at sea, has but little answered the design. For these people, long inured to the land service and now compelled when stiff with age and accidents to enter upon a life of quite a different nature, are so disheartened, that in bad weather, when ordered to go aloft, they will fall all along, and submit to your utmost resentment, rather than stir a foot in what they apprehend so hazardous an undertaking. And the Russian population in general are incredibly dispirited, partly through the despotic power of their superiors; as also by their own mean, sordid way of living, being much addicted to salts and acids and extremely afflicted with the scurvy; and so accustomed to *bagnios* that unless they have recourse at least once a week to cleanse themselves, they are almost consumed with vermin. But of the last disservice in this article, is that their religion enjoins a strict observation of three annual fasts, amounting in the whole to fifteen weeks, besides every Wednesday and Friday throughout the year; and so tenacious is the ignorant superstitious multitude of this less essential part, that when great numbers of sick have been landed from aboard the Russian fleet, especially in these fasting seasons, and the Tsar has ordered a provision of fresh meat and set a guard to prevent the introducing all other support, many have actually perished rather than violate their ill-informed consciences in eating of prohibited viands. And although the Tsar, in his private opinion highly condemns this impolitic custom; yet perceiving the strong attachment of the populace, he forbears to abolish it by public edict; but underhand endeavours to overthrow [it] by turning it into ridicule, with many other extravagances in their religion and customs; and herein is seconded by many of the modern Russ both in the army and the navy, that have been abroad in the world. Notwithstanding, so little progress is made, that scarce one in a hundred amongst the under-officers and seamen, will, unless by pure compulsion, break in upon this established notion; so strong an impression they receive from their priests, inculcating under pain of damnation, an avoidance of such innovations. However, this abstinence emaciates them and mightily aggravates their dejection of spirit; taking away both strength and inclination to any work that requires activity and force of body; and as the case stands, I can't see that anything, unless long trading voyages, will serve to eradicate this bigotry out of their minds.

[During] one or two summers, [on] some few days cruisers, continuing a good while at sea, took several prizes; and thereby the Russ common sailors, permitted to taste of the sweets of success, were brought to a greater improvement than ordinary.

XXIV. THE TSAR'S BALTIC INTERESTS.

About ten years since,[1] the Tsar would have willingly condescended to deliver up all his conquests, upon condition of reserving to himself St. Petersburg; and rather than part with this he determined to abide the last extremities. The land about this city is generally morass and wilderness, producing little or nothing for the support of man; and though the subsistence of such populous places requires the cultivation of the adjacent ground, yet the Tsar will not give leave to clear or meliorate the soil, but on the contrary has issued a strict prohibition against the cutting up of the least tree or shrub within twenty, and in some parts within thirty, miles thereof. For St. Petersburg, being built on several islands and standing on a vast extent of ground, will not possibly admit of fortification.[2] Besides, the buildings, being mostly of wood, are liable to be burned on any sudden incursion; and, therefore, its main security lies in rendering the avenues impassable, and this also suits admirably well with the temper of the Russian soldiery, ever reputed better at ambuscade, or defence of a place where they lie covered, than in the bravery of an open assault. A year or two after this, he insisted upon Viborg also as a convenient barrier; and still his ambition being progressive as his power, so his demands increased.

A little before the consummation of the late war,

---

[1] *I.e.* in 1714.
[2] 'The building of St. Petersburg seems almost like a freak. . . . It was nothing but a costly and useless toy. The fortress on which so much money and so much life were spent then, as now, protected nothing. Its guns could never reach the enemy unless the town had been previously taken' (Schuyler, ii. p. 12).

the common subject of discourse amongst the men of penetration in his navy was the method of employing his fleet in time of peace. Since otherwise, a final period would be put to his nursery for education of seamen, the chief expedient proposed was that particular care be taken in treaties of commerce with foreign powers to obtain the privilege of exporting, in his own ships, the product of his own dominions. But then came under debate how far Great Britain and Holland would give in to such a concession, considering his capacity of manning and victualling his ships at much cheaper rates than they. To this might be added, if the Tsar should succeed in his pretensions of a passage for his ships, toll free, through the Sound;[1] on how much easier terms might he then import into his own country the merchandise of different nations: as has been already in part, to the detriment of our navigation, exemplified in the time that Sweden, possessed only of the sea coasts, enjoyed that exemption. Whereas the Tsar, now in the possession of the principal part, entirely removing the staple of the trade from Archangel, has drawn in a manner, the whole commerce of his dominions into the Baltic; and necessitated the general system of Russian imports and exports; an inconsiderable deduction allowed to pass through the Sound: and this may in time be farther aggravated, if he succeed in his canal of communication betwixt the Volkoff and Neva, and grasps into his hands the Persian trade. As all these things conduce to aggrandise his beloved St. Petersburg, unless they are found absolutely impracticable, they are sure to be prosecuted with the utmost vigour. And assuredly he wants a port in the hithermost parts of the Baltic for the bringing these designs to maturity, that are as yet but in

[1] See note on the Sound dues (*post*, p. 117).

embryo; as also for a commodious reception of his ships, when the season too far advanced will not allow of their proceeding to the ports already in his possession.

XXV. NECESSITY OF SEA-EXPERIENCE FOR THE TSAR'S NAVY.

Just upon the conclusion of the late peace [1] with Sweden, it was hotly talked of that the Tsar would send a squadron of men-of-war, through the Sound and British Channel up the Straits into the Mediterranean; and travelling in person by land meet them at Venice. Of a truth, there are men of towering spirits, in no mean characters in his navy, that, knowing his boundless ambition, use their utmost efforts to soothe this principle with the view of making their private advantage of it. Since if war with the Turk should ensue the command of a squadron in the Mediterranean would furnish them with a fine opportunity of making their fortunes, and afterwards of retiring: for notwithstanding the glitter of their present state and outward appearance of satisfaction, they necessarily regard Russia no otherwise than as an unavoidable prison. Some I have known so sanguine in their expectations this way, as to take upon 'em to justify the Tsar's right to the Island of Tobago,[2] in the West Indies, by virtue of

---

[1] Of Nystadt, $\frac{\text{August 30}}{\text{September 10}}$, 1721.

[2] Tobago was 'discovered by Columbus in 1498. William, Earl of Pembroke, in 1528, obtained a grant of this island with that of Barbuda. About 1632 some Zealanders, trading with the West India Islands, gave such a favourable report of Tobago in particular that a company of merchants undertook to settle it, and gave it the name of New Walcheren, from one of the islands of their province. The Spaniards exterminated the new colony. James, Duke of Courland, sent a colony to Tobago, who settled upon Great Courland Bay, and erected a small fort with a town.

his present possession of Courland; and would expatiate on the manifold advantages that would accrue to that Prince upon making a settlement there.

After all, the Tsar lies under an absolute necessity of enterprising something to improve his men. And when the late war was drawing to an end, some of his grandees expected upon a peace, they should be obliged to turn merchants; and either building or taking ships, upon certain conditions, of the Tsar, send them out on trading voyages with double complement of men. And should they bring such a thing to bear, one inconvenience would undoubtedly attend it; when their men had learned how to get their bread, and seen the preferable manner of living in other countries, they would infallibly desert, as many did in 1715 from ships that wintered in Norway, though that region affords but little temptation; and the strict alliance then subsisting between the Tsar and the King of Denmark must lay 'em under apprehensions of being surrendered if reclaimed.

XXVI. THE RUSSIAN BALTIC FLEET.

The Russian navy on the Baltic side, consisted in its present state of thirty sail of line-of-battle ships, and six on the stocks a-building, with oak timber in the province of Kazan for thirty more; the labour of several years; besides frigates, snows,

---

The Duke's title was confirmed by Charles II., but disputed by the Dutch. Upon the extinction of the Ketteler family, Dukes of Courland, the fief of the island reverted to the crown of England in 1737, and by the Treaty, concluded in Paris in 1763, it was ceded in full right to Great Britain.' In May, 1781, it was taken by the French. In 1793 it was retaken by the British, by whom it is still retained (Fullarton's *Gazetteer of the World*, Edinburgh, (?) 1851, vol. vii.).

prahms and bomb-vessels. All the Tsar's galleys, as yet built on the Baltic, are of fir; occasioned by the difficulty of bringing oak timber to St. Petersburg; but within these two last years since the Tsar resolved on the Caspian expedition, oak timber has been felled, and moulded, in the place above mentioned, for 100 galleys, and for carriages of 200 large cannon. Experience confirms that his best fir built ships will not last above seven years; and even some of oak timber want rebuilding at the expiration of eight. Peradventure this date might be something extended, if, in felling, due regard was had to the season of the year and age of the trees. But having hitherto been extremely profuse, they are not compelled to range at a great distance in quest of proper trees; and have generally in winter ten or twelve thousand Tartar inhabitants, with three or four thousand horses, employed in drawing the timber out of the woods to the bank of the Volga. This river in its course, rolling through vast tracts of land covered all winter with perpetual snows, that dissolve in the spring and cause an inundation overflowing great part of the country, enriching the soil, and furnishing the inhabitants with a fine opportunity of bringing, by water, to their own doors, all necessaries for the ensuing year, yet, thereby, necessitates the Tsar's people to lay up their timber in prodigious piles, to prevent its being carried away, at the ascent, and by the force of the torrent; and, being thus exposed to wet and dry, much of what has cost the Tsar some money and many men and horses their lives, becomes rotten before it is put aboard the *strouds*,[1] flat vessels for transporta-

---

[1] Charnock spells this word 'stroeg.' Speaking of the insurrection in Russia (1666-1671) of Stenka Razin, he says: '... the navy of the insurgents was composed of stroegs, or barks, besides other vessels, &c.' (*Hist. Marine Architecture*, vol. ii. p. 356).

UNDER PETER THE GREAT

tion. Every piece, when moulded, is stamped with its proper name and loaded when the water is at highest. This, at Tver, 130 English miles above Moscow, happens in May, at Kazan in June, and at Astrakhan in July. The Tsar's own vessels and people for several years transported these materials; but, of late, undertakers engage to convey, at certain price, the timber of a ship of so many guns, from Kazan to the Ladoga Lake; for instance of a 60-gun ship, for fourteen or fifteen thousand roubles. They track or warp as the shores allow, up the Volga to the town of Tver, and there, striking off, hold on their course north-west up Tver river, and one river more, till the waters near Turgock and Vishni-Volochok growing small and frequent shallows occurring, notwithstanding the help of sluices in some difficult parts, are unable to proceed in the latter end of the summer. All this way they go against the stream; but in the spring, at the return of high water, pursuing their voyage near Beonets, about twenty-three English miles from Novgorod, are let by a canal into a little river, issuing into the lake Juna from whence the Volkoff commencing, they pass it down, under a handsome bridge at Novgorod and descend into the Ladoga Lake. There the timber is unladen into the Tsar's vessels, such as *croyers*, *schootes*,[1] *careybashes*, appointed to carry it to St. Petersburg. The navigation on this lake is very difficult by reason of the deep water, few harbours, sorry shipping, and inexperience of the Russian seamen; and great is the danger in passing the three falls, at the entrance into the Neva. So that many vessels are yearly lost, to the exceeding detriment of St. Petersburg

---

[1] 'Schoote' is the Dutch 'schoot' of Charnock (*Hist. Mar. Archit.*, vol. ii. p. 189). The word is spelled *schuit* in Dutch (see Calisch's *Dictionary*).

in point of merchandise, and especially of provisions, all supplies coming this way. And the accomplishing the canal of communication betwixt the Volkoff and Neva, on which the Tsar is so intent, is the only expedient to remove these fatal inconveniences. It is supposed the Tsar designed to have always in condition of service, forty sail of ships from 50 to 100 guns; and ten years being the utmost allowance for their duration, he will be obliged to build two new ships, and rebuild two others every year in order to keep up his number; and if he has ten frigates, must alternately build or rebuild a frigate year by year. As little as his fleet has been at sea, several ships have been cast away; and as they can do him little service, unless they appear more abroad, so their risk must increase in proportion.

If the Tsar attains to his aim of having forty ships of line of battle, in his harbours on the Baltic, he will be more than a match for the Dane or Swede. Shipbuilders he has enough, as likewise flag officers of every degree; and the inconsiderable number of captains and lieutenants wanting may be supplied at the shortest warning by advancing some of his own people, that have long thought all foreigners superfluous and make a jest of their experience. Many of this kind have been preferred, within three years last past,[1] since the Tsar, conceiving too high an opinion of his naval power, and the capacity of his subjects, has been less severe in examining into the behaviour and abilities of these youths; and this had led their instructors into a growing evil of giving certificates before a sufficient acquisition of knowlege. Under-officers may be made of the best sailors; and their list again filled up by breaking some regiments of soldiers, accord-

[1] *I.e.* since the Peace of Nystadt.

ing to the known method obtaining in Russia. By these means each ship may have its full complement, amounting to $\frac{1}{4}$ or $\frac{1}{3}$ more than the English [1] establishment in like cases; their way being there to pick up all that belong to the sea and then divide 'em in proportion, as far as they will go; employing the reduced serjeants and corporals for gunners and bombardiers; and yet generally are obliged to send out fewer ships than at first they designed. The half the ships' companies are soldiers; and the greater part of the residue such as, a year or two before, underwent a translation from soldiers to seamen; so that, often in a 54-gun ship, whose common appointment is 400 men, when the upper and under officers, guard-marines,[2] and cabin-boys are deducted, not 40, except she is a flag, nay, not 30 are to be found that deserve the character of able sailors at their going out to sea.

In the Russian Navy are found some foreigners

---

[1] The complements of English ships in the early part of the eighteenth century were—

1st rates	. 96 to 100 guns;	706 to 800 men
2nd rates	. 84 „ 90 „	524 „ 640 „
3rd rates	. 66 „ 80 „	390 „ 476 „
4th rates	. 46 „ 60 „	230 „ 346 „
5th rates	. 26 „ 44 „	135 „ 150 „
6th rates	. 24 „	110 „

(*An Essay on the Navy*, in two parts, by the author of the *Seamen's Case* [John Dennis], London, 1702).

[2] 'Guard-marines,' from the French *Gardes-marines*, the designation applied in the seventeenth and eighteenth centuries to young officers in the Royal Navy of France, as being nominally gentlemen 'privates' in the King's Guard. 'C'est à cette époque [c. 1673] que Colbert créa, sous le nom de compagnies de *gardes-marines*, une pépinière d'officiers de vaisseau; les compagnies comprenaient deux cents gentilshommes, répartis entre les trois ports de Brest, Rochefort et Toulon. Les jeunes gens y étaient admis de seize à vingt ans, au bon plaisir du roi et sans examens. La seule condition à remplir pour l'admission était d'appartenir à la noblesse' (Maurice Loir, *La Marine Française*, Paris, 1893, p. 46). See *ante*, p. 55.

of worth, as appears in the course of this narrative; but, if a precise calculation, and only men of experience and skill in the languages [be] included, their number is diminutively small; and these are still the less formidable through party divisions and prejudices, as consisting of nations different in their taste, views, interests and manner of living.

There are also some men of capacity amongst the Russians, but as to the generality of these, in quality of lieutenants, foreigners ever desire to leave 'em ashore; seeing in good weather their pride is insupportable, taking great state upon them, and arrogating much attendance; but in bad weather, or any extremity, are sick abed, when they should be serviceable.

If the Russian fleet is attacked in their own roads, lying at anchor in an advantageous posture, the water smooth and their bodies well secured from small shot, and their commanders are men of resolution, exposing their persons and seeming insensible of danger, then the common Russ, forming their judgment from the officers' intrepid aspect, apprehend the peril to be less than it really is, and will stand their ground, traverse the guns, and make a handsome defence, ever a Russian's masterpiece; and still so much the braver as being sure of the galleys, in great numbers, to assist them, and annoy the enemy, as opportunity presents.

Few if any ships in the world are able to wrong the Russian, especially those built at St. Petersburg, if well manned, in the qualification of excellent sailing; and they are incomparably provided with masts, sails, anchors, cables, and cordage, all the proper product of Russia; and the prime of everything is picked out for the use of the royal navy. Every commander has power to condemn and demand new; and the quality and quantity being left to him, occasioned formerly an extravagant expense; and still this article runs high. This valuable advantage of good sailing is of the less service to the Tsar, through an unreasonable prepossession in favour of his officers and people, arising from a long series of success, and inducing him to send out every year more ships to sea than he is in a condition to man with sailors of any experience; and if pursuing or pursued by an enemy, they will never be able to manage their sails, nor work their ships so quick as is necessary in a chase; much less be prepared for all winds and weather. And, though the season there for ships being at sea is comparatively short, and storms less frequent in summer; yet they must take their chance, and will many times meet with variable winds and changeable weather. However, the Tsar's eager thirst after fame will not permit him to be convinced of his error. If a Russian offers to undeceive him, he apparently runs the risk of being branded with the odious name of 'Old Russian,' one disaffected to his Majesty's glorious administration. Nor will this Prince suffer a native of his dominions to enter the lists of comparison in point of maritime skill. If a foreigner presumes, his courage or capacity is called in question; or at least he is thought to entertain too mean an opinion of the Russian improvement; though any man that has seen the condition their ships are in at sea, in a strong gale of wind, must readily allow a much inferior force might easily attack and destroy them; provided there was sea room sufficient to prevent their escaping into their harbours. For at such a juncture, though under no extraordinary apprehensions, and consequently in free exercise of thought, they never could manage their ships as they ought. And how much less will they be able to do it, after ten or twelve days' continuance at sea, when many are sea sick, or otherwise in ill state of health, and the rest thunderstruck with the terror of an approaching engagement, under various disadvantages in an element disagreeable to far the major part and the distraction heightened by the everlasting animosities and emulation subsisting betwixt land and sea officers and their people. The officers from a sense of their people's inexperience will be fearful of opening their ports or loosening their guns, lest by ill steerage, or other mismanagement, the sea run in at their portholes, or the guns break loose and endanger their sinking, especially amongst the Russians, whose known property is ever to recoil from danger, even when immediate presence of mind is requisite to repel an otherwise unavoidable ruin. And the people construing the officers' caution in the worst sense, will quite lose the spirit they have, and when they come to engage do but little execution, neither firing so quick, nor sure as they might, through confusion and despair of success. And even in calm moderate weather, when the people are in condition to behave something better, yet the enemy has great advantage through the badness of their powder; and commanders acquainted with the hazard they run, above all things dread the blowing up of their ships, through the fear, ignorance, and confusion of the undisciplined multitude. The Russian ships of war have never[1] been in any action worth taking notice of, and always four to one, when aught of that kind offered. What method the Tsar will take to instruct his people time alone can

---

[1] As before remarked in the notes, the battle at Hangö Head was not a sea-fight, and was not fought between the Russian and Swedish navies, but between the Russian *galley fleet* and the Swedish *skärgårds fleet* (*Peter der Grosse*, by Professor Alexander Brückner, of Dorpat University, Berlin, 1879, p. 421).

ascertain; since the usage of foreigners in Russia is too notorious for any to go there unless incapacitated to live in other countries, and the want of a due provision for men disabled by age or accidents is still an additional discouragement.

For two or three years past the Tsar, unwilling to omit any opportunity of improving his seamen, has supplied the foreign merchants at St. Petersburg with vessels to carry on their trade from thence to Kronslot, Viborg, and Narva, on the following terms. These vessels, being chiefly *evers*, sailing with one mast, are appraised and an inventory of everything belonging to them with their proper value taken. The merchant receiving the vessel gets an Englishman or Hollander, generally one dismissed out of the Tsar's service, to command her, with four or five Russ common sailors; and employing her to the latter end of the summer or as long as his occasions require, then delivers her over to the officers of the yard, where the vessel and furniture are again surveyed and compared with the former inventory and all the damages sustained made good by the merchant. Several of the Russian merchants also voluntarily took vessels on the same condition and others by compulsion. In 1722, the inhabitants of the conquered cities and towns lying on the Baltic had the same offer made them which the merchants of Riga accepted, and receiving some larger vessels, traded into divers ports in that sea; and were it not for the obstacle of the Sound duties,[1] had probably appeared before now in other parts of the world.

---

[1] *Sound Dues.*—From the beginning of the fifteenth century Denmark had levied at Helsingör (Elsinore) on all vessels passing through the Sound a tax known as the 'Sound Dues,' her right to which had been recognised by treaties with other Powers. Vessels belonging to the six Hanse towns—Lübeck, Hamburg, Rostock,

In the entrance of the year 1723 the Tsar, accompanied by the General-Admiral, Commodore Gosler, Captain Villebois and some few of inferior rank, returning from the Caspian expedition, and the rest of the sea officers present in that service wintering at Astrakhan, orders were issued out for getting a considerable number of ships and some galleys in readiness for sea ; and being unwilling to let so many ships lie useless in his havens, as having more already than he was able to man, besides several abuilding, part whereof near ready to launch, he determined for the improvement of his seamen to send some of them up the Mediterranean, with merchandise that might turn to account, designing also if possible to sell some of those supernumerary vessels. For the English shipbuilders have always used their utmost endeavours to put the Tsar out of conceit with all ships but such as are built by themselves or the Russ builders at St. Petersburg. And when any others fall into their hands to be repaired they take especial care to omit the ornamental part, whereby they serve as foils to the ships built in Russia, surpassing all others in the beauty of their carved works and richness of their gildings ; full scope being given herein to the builder's fancy. The Devonshire, L'Espérance and New Kronslot, three ships brought from Holland, were pitched upon for this purpose ; and ordered to take in tar, soap, bees-

---

Stralsund, Wismar, and Lüneburg—were exempt; as also were those of Stettin, Kolberg, and Kammin. To Swedish, Dutch, English, and French vessels a reduction was granted. In 1853 the dues brought in a revenue of 2,530,000 thalers (about 350,000*l.*). The United States made a treaty with Denmark, and decided not to pay dues in future. A conference of nearly all the European Powers met at Copenhagen in January 1856. A treaty was made in April 1857 by the terms of which Denmark, in return for a sum of 30,476,325 Danish reichsthalers, agreed to the abolition of the Sound Dues (Meyer's *Konversations-Lexikon*, vol. xvi. 1897).

wax, candles, cartridge paper, ammunition, small arms and cannon of various dimensions. For at Olonetz, not far from the Ladoga Lake, the Tsar has great ironworks. Ore,[1] timber and all necessaries, are the natural product of the country, provisions and labour cheap, and foreigners being established to instruct the Russians, one of whom, an Englishman and anchor-smith, makes all the anchors for the navy. By these means they are now arrived to a great perfection in casting of cannon, making of all sorts of small arms and ammunition, so that a modern cannon carrying 18 pound shot weighs no more than a 12 pounder cast ten years ago. These commodities will answer in most countries abroad, as likewise cordage and other naval stores, reserved for exportation in his own bottoms. By the Tsar's especial orders the commanders and all above mates were to be Russians; and Jacob Savage, lieutenant of the Ormonde in its[2] voyage to Venice in 1717, born of Dutch parents turned Russians at Archangel, was to have the chief command.

XXVII. QUESTIONS RELATING TO OFFICERS

The Tsar, as before related, having appointed three degrees of captains as to salary, some disputes arose on the article of precedency, during his absence in the Caspian expedition, and being referred to the College were decided in favour of the officers allowed the larger pay, such as are above described by the title of first rank captains, without regard to the date of their commissions all expressly drawn in the same tenour and form. But the Tsar at his return gave it the contrary way, saying, 'I

---

[1] MS. 'Oar.'   [2] *Sic* in MS.

will reserve to myself the liberty of granting what pay I please to each captain ; but the senior commission shall always have the post of honour.' At this time also the master shipbuilders, discontented with their former allotment of place, found means to procure an alteration, whereby rank was assigned 'em equal to a captain-commodore in the navy and a brigadier in the army.

Several foreigners, arriving at St. Petersburg whilst the Tsar was abroad in his Persian enterprise, now in his return addressed [him] for employment. The Lord Duffus soon had the character of rear-admiral conferred upon him ; and received as reported a year's pay in advance with a promise of being made at the end of the campaign Intendant of the Maritime Affairs ashore, according to the method of France.[1] Vice-Admiral Gordon, by the Tsar's order, had some time before engaged one Mr. Cooper, formerly storekeeper in His Majesty's yard at Portsmouth, to go over and serve the Tsar under promise of several hundred pounds per annum salary. To this man instructions and proper remittances of money were lent to induce several English officers to accompany him ; but living beyond his abilities, he grew necessitous, and little progress was made in engaging commanders. Some few articled and were dispatched to Holland, where money and credit failing they suffered much and proceeded no farther. But Cooper went to St. Petersburg and, whilst waiting a year for the Tsar's return,

---

[1] *Intendant de Marine.*—' Dans les ports l'intendant était omnipotent. Tout dépendait de lui, justice, police, finances, magasins, ateliers, construction, garde, entretien, mouvements des vaisseaux. Il avait, en vérité, près de lui un commandant de la marine et, au-dessous, un capitaine de port, mais il ne leur laissait que le soin de veiller à la sûreté de l'arsenal ; il était véritablement le chef ou, selon l'expression de Colbert, "l'homme de Sa Majesté"' (Maurice Loir, *La Marine Française*, p. 40).

differed with Mr. Gordon his patron, so that at that Prince's return he met with a very indifferent reception; though the English gentlemen had pressed the Tsar to entertain this man as the properest person for regulating his naval affairs according to the establishments in the docks and yards in England.

The Russian fleet, being according to order ready to put to sea, upon the repeated complaint of the officers that they had not sailors sufficient to man the number of ships proposed, the Tsar perceiving the effective men fall greatly short of the lists given in, resolved to leave some behind; but as he determined to have all his flag-officers to accompany him, probably to inspect into their capacities, the ships when reduced were not numerous enough to allow each admiral his proper division. Admiral Cruys therefore had leave to stay behind and the vice-admirals had orders to hoist rear-admirals' flags, and rear-admirals to wear broad pennants.[1] Some offence was taken thereat, but it was the Tsar's absolute pleasure and the only expedient he could find to remedy this inconveniency. Accordingly he sailed with four and twenty ships of line of battle having four flags hoisted and eight flag-officers aboard: and now for the first time the General-Admiral hoisted and sailed under the Jack or Union flag[2] hitherto having worn the white: and

---

[1] See *ante*, p. 18, note.
[2] The English and Dutch fleets were divided into three divisions or squadrons—the Red, the White, and the Blue. Peter copied the arrangement of the Dutch, from whom also he had borrowed the colours of the Russian ensign. 'Il est tout à la Hollande; il adopte son pavillon, rouge, blanc et bleu, en changeant seulement l'ordre des couleurs' (Waliszewski, *Pierre le Grand*, p. 69). In the English navy the order used to be—1, Red; 2, Blue; 3, White; this was changed during the Commonwealth to 1, Red; 2, White; 3, Blue, an arrangement lasting till 1864. For a long time there was no Admiral of the Red, officers senior to the Admirals of the White flying the Union Jack. The distinc-

Vice-Admiral Sievers was on board the same ship, as he always is, when Count Apraxin commands. After forming lines of battle and a variety of exercise, they put into Revel and Råger Wik, and at the last place the Tsar laid the first stone of the haven designed to be carried out in earnest the ensuing winter, unless obstructed by the mildness of the season; for, except it freezes hard enough to bear all sorts of carriage quite across the Bay, it is impossible to work to any purpose. At the end of this expedition the fleet returned to Kronslot where at their arrival the Tsar ordered them all to hoist their proper flags; and several days were spent in masquerades and different diversions.

Upon accepting the advantageous proposals made by the Persian Ambassador,[1] the Tsar's views this way seemed to cool and the three ships bound for Venice were ordered to unrig and winter at Revel; whereby this Prince's claim to an exemption from the duties payable at passing the Sound remains undetermined. How far he intended to have tried the King of Denmark's resolution, had he not been allured by so fair an offer to the eastward, is not my province to pronounce.

tion, Admiral of the Red, was established as a substantive distinction in 1805. Sir George Rooke flew the Union at the main at Vigo in 1702, and at Malaga in 1704. Sir George Byng flew the same flag on the coast of Sicily in 1718 (J. K. Laughton, 'The Heraldry of the Sea—Ensigns, Colours, and Flags,' *Journal R.U.S.I.*, February 28, 1879). These instances were, of course, known to the English officers in Peter's fleet, and a knowledge of them induced him to copy the practice.

[1] Peter started from Moscow on his Persian expedition in May 1722. At Astrakhan he embarked on the Caspian Sea, on which Apraxin was the first officer to hoist an admiral's flag. Peter returned to Moscow in December 1722. Hostilities formally ceased in September 1723 (Voltaire, *Œuvres*, xvi. p. 619, note).

XXVIII. VARIOUS WORKS IN HAND— CONCLUDING REMARKS.

In October Captain-Commodore Lane returned from inspecting the new canal of communication betwixt the Volkoff and Neva, for the frost setting in obliged to desist from all works that require digging. The dock and basin at Kronslot having been carried on for some years past, with great application, were now advanced so far that a part of the stonework was done. Both these are to be paved and walled to the surface of the water with large square stone from Narva; and above with choice oak timber and plank, prepared at Kazan two years ago, with some other of very large dimensions, for dock-gates, drawbridge, &c. Contiguous to the island beyond the outermost fortifications lies a place of flat shoal[1] water, of half a mile extent. In the front thereof, where deep water commences, Captain-Commodore Lane was ordered to drive in piles, and sink chests in order to raise an artificial bank; and the intermediate space between this mound and the shore was to be the receptacle of prodigious quantities of earth, thrown up out of the dock, basin and adjacent canals, at present incommoding the other works; but, deposited there, would make it firm land and serve the Tsar's design to add some fortification to seaward. But as soon as the ice grew strong enough he was to depart from Kronslot and push on the works at Råger Wik in conjunction with Colonel Lubrass, an engineer. This gentleman has also the direction of a new canal of about six English miles in length, commencing at Strelna Muse, where the Tsar is building a fine palace, and ending just within the

[1] MS. 'Shole.'

mouth of the river Neva, about three miles below St. Petersburg. The Tsar herein proposes a double advantage: one that ships of moderate draught of water in their passage from Kronslot to St. Petersburg may shun the troublesome bar that much retards their course in westerly winds, which commonly blow there; the other, he hopes it will give such a refluent vent to their waters as will in a good degree secure them from future inundations.

This year two ships were rebuilt, the Pearl at Revel and Poltava at St. Petersburg; and two condemned, the Strafford and Victoria, both formerly bought in England; the bottom of [the] Narva blown up in 1715 was also weighed and removed at a great but necessary expense, because she lay just in the way of other ships' anchorage. Three ships were launched this summer, the Cruiser, a frigate of 30 guns, the St. Michael, mounting 50 guns, but every way exceeding the dimensions of a ship of that force, projected by the Tsar and Mr. Browne and built by the latter; proposed to outsail any ship whatever, and said to be designed for the Tsar; not to come in line of battle in time of action, but [be] stationed amongst the light frigates, the better to view the posture of both the fleets, and be the more distinctly seen, when she makes the proper signals. Some years ago the Tsar espoused a quite different notion of shipping, alleging that as the waves in the Baltic, when the wind blows hard, swell not to so great a height as in the ocean, but make what seamen call short seas; consequently shorter built ships would have the advantage in sailing on this sea beyond others of greater length. I have heard him strenuously maintain this point of theory, about twelve years ago; but experience has since convinced him of his mistake; and at this time he allows them their full length, or rather exceeds, as exemplified in the present instance and likewise in two 96-gun ships now upon the stocks, measuring longer than the Royal Sovereign.[1] The third ship launched was the[2] Le Firme, hauled up in 1720, being now made a new ship. The Slutelburg is appointed to be hauled up this winter for rebuilding; for till the dock is perfected, there is no way to come at and rebuild their bottoms. When, therefore, in this narrative any other ships have been said to be rebuilt, it is to be understood only of the part above the water's edge. And the Tsar is so much the more desirous of finishing the dock because it will save the excessive expense of hauling up ships on dry land, and likewise as the ships built of oak timber at St. Petersburg—the only ones he values —are considerably increased in number. So several of 'em waxing old, some already, and others soon, will want an entire rebuilding. This summer, likewise, strict orders were published, forbidding the access of all persons not immediately in the service, to the haven of Kronslot; and the officers on guard were commanded to apprehend any that should make an attempt of that kind.

In November Mr. Cooper, after two years' attendance and reducement to poverty, was fixed in the management of the naval stores, at the salary of 600 roubles for the first year, with a Russian promise of performing his first agreement amounting to four times that sum for the future; on condition of his accomplishing what he pretended to.

---

[1] The author probably refers to the Royal Sovereign, on board which Sir George Rooke hoisted his flag in 1702. Derrick (*Memoirs, &c.*, p. 260) gives the dimensions of a ship of 100 guns for the year 1719 as follows: length on gun-deck, 174 ft.; length of keel for tonnage, 140 ft. 7 in.; breadth, extreme, 50 ft.; depth in hold, 19 ft. 2 in.; burthen in tons, 1869 (see note 3, p. 10).

[2] See note 1, p. 30.

Deductions in the officers' pay and several new regulations were made in the beginning of this campaign. Gordon's and Saunders' additional allowance from the Cabinet, or privy purse, [were] taken off. Many were uneasy at the deduction of 25 per cent., and others grumbled at dropping the thirteenth month's pay, but all the answer they could get was, if any officer was dissatisfied he might have his dismission at the end of the campaign. However, some regard was shown, on these two heads, to such as contracted abroad ; and the 25 per cent. seems to be suspended till the commencement of the present new year, 1724. This suspension is only to foreigners, the Russians having paid it for the year 1723.

On a thorough collation of particulars, I am fully of opinion though the number of his[1] ships is increased, yet his seamen, properly so called, are not more numerous, within these last four years. And the vast charge he is yearly at to discipline his men and keep up his fleet to its present height, whilst little or no service is done him in return of such expense, must inevitably exhaust his treasures and render him less formidable. All future designs and expectations must abide in a state of inexecution till his affairs in Asia stand on a less precarious footing ; and should he in his turn meet with adverse fortune, it would past all peradventure ruin many, if not most of his great undertakings.

XXIX. *LIST OF RUSSIAN SHIPS IN* 1724.

A list of the Russian fleet capable of going to sea the beginning of the summer 1724 before any more are launched, in case seamen can be found to man

[1] Peter's.

them, and the expedition be not far from the Tsar's own coasts. Those marked with a cross are old and crazy, and those marked N3 can't carry sail when it blows anything hard, and consequently unfit for distant enterprises.

Ships' Names	No. of Guns	
Hangö Head	90	N3
Lesnoy	90	N3
Fredrikstadt	90	
St. Peter	90	
St. Andrew	90	
Freedmaker	90	
North Eagle (*Severnoi Oril*)	80	
St. Alexander	70	x
Neptunus	70	x
Le Firme	70	
Revell	64	
Moscow	64	x ⎫ 'Tis supposed these
Ingermanland	64	x ⎭ go no more to sea.
Isaak Victoria	64	
Astrakhan	64	
Katharina	64	
Marlborough	64	
Pantaloon Victoria	64	N3
Devonshire	60	
Viborg	60	x
Poltava	54	
Prince Eugene	54	
St. Michael	50	
Pearl	50	
Britannia	50	x
Randolph	50	
Ormonde	50	x
Arundel	48	x
L'Espérance	44	
Wachtmeister	44	x
Amsterdam Galley	36	
Crown de Lieft	36	
Cruiser	36	
Samson	32	
Stora Phœnix	30	

And several others of less force.

XXX. LIST OF OFFICERS IN THE RUSSIAN NAVY IN THE BALTIC

A List of the Officers that have occasionally been named in this Relation.[1]

Names	Nation	Post
Antufioff	Russia	Captain-Lieutenant
Apraxin, Frederick [2]	Russia	General-Admiral
Apraxin, Alexander	Russia	Captain-Lieutenant
Armitage, Samuel	England	Captain
Arseenoff	Russia	Captain-Lieutenant
Baker, William	England	Captain, dismissed in 1717
Basheloff	Russia	Captain-Lieutenant
Batting, William	England	Captain, dead in 1720
Bents, Peter	Holland	Captain
Besemacher, Peter	Denmark	Captain, has the direction of the pilots at Riga
Blorey, John	Holland	Captain, equipage master at Astrachan
Bohen	Hamburg	Captain, dismissed in 1721
Brant, Isaac	Norway	Captain
Bredale, Peter	Norway	Captain-Commodore
Callmecoff	Russia	Captain
Carabin	Russia	Captain
Chapezan, Jacob	Hanover	Captain
Cronenburg	Holland	Captain
Cruys, Cornelius	Norway	Admiral of the Blue, dead in 1715
Deane, John	England	Captain, dismissed in 1722
Degruter	Holland	Captain, dismissed 1714
Delap, John	Ireland	Captain
Ducy	Holland	Captain-Lieutenant, dismissed in 1717, since engaged as Lieutenant
Eckoff, Clays	Denmark	Captain, has the direction of the pilots in the Gulf of Finland
Edwards, Benjamin	England	Captain, dismissed 1717

[1] Several names mentioned in the body of the MS. are not included in this list—for example, Vitus Bering, Cramer (or Kremer), De Cour.

[2] Really Feodore (see note, p. 77).

Names	Nation	Post
Falkenberg, Mathias	Sweden (supposed)	Captain
Fitch	England	Captain, dismissed 1715
Golovin, Nicholas	Russia	Captain
Gordon, Thomas	North Britain	Vice-Admiral of the Red
Gosler, Martin	Holstein	Captain-Commodore
Griese	Lübeck	Captain, dismissed 1718
Harboe, Peter	Denmark	Captain-Lieutenant
Hay, William	North Britain	Captain, dismissed 1724
Hoogstraten, Adrian	Holland	Captain
Huyck	Denmark	Captain, dead in 1718
Kasheloff	Russia	Captain
Knee, Michael	Denmark	Captain, dismissed 1721
Lobanoff	Russia	Captain-Lieutenant
Lane, Edward	Wales	Captain-Commodore and Engineer
Laurence, James	England	Captain
Lenoy	France	Captain, dead in 1721
Little, Robert	England	Captain
Masnoy	Russia	Captain
Menshikoff	Russia	Vice-Admiral of the White
Mishecoff	Russia	Captain
Muconoff	Russia	Captain
Nelson	England	Captain, dead in 1717
Nobel	Denmark	Captain, dismissed 1719
Paddon, George	New England	Rear-Admiral of the White, dead in 1718
Papagoy	New York	Captain, dead in 1718
Rue, Thomas	England	Captain, dismissed 1717
Savage, Jacob	Russia	Captain-Lieutenant
Saunders, Thomas	England	Rear-Admiral of the White
Schelling	Denmark	Captain, broke in 1718
Scheltinga, Wybrant	Holland	Rear-Admiral of the Red, dead in 1718
Serocold, John	England	Captain-Lieutenant
Sievers, Peter	Denmark	Vice-Admiral of the Blue
Sinavin, Ivan	Russia	Captain-Commodore
Sinavin, Nahum	Russia	Rear-Admiral of the Blue
Simpson, Andrew	North Britain	Captain, dismissed 1714
Squerscoff	Russia	Captain-Lieutenant
Stegman	Germany	Captain, dead in 1721
Stubbs	England	Captain, dismissed 1723
Thofft, Lodwick	Holland	Captain, dismissed 1718
Trane, Antony	Norway	Captain, Equipage Master at Revel
Tressel, Peter	Holland	Captain

Names	Nation[1]	Post
Turnhoud, William	Holland	Captain, dismissed 1721
Urquhart, Adam	North Britain	Captain-Lieutenant, killed in 1719
Vandergun	Holland	Captain, dismissed in 1720, now soliciting justice
Van Gent	Holland	Captain, dismissed 1722
Van Hofft	Brabant	Rear-Admiral of the Red
Vianen, John	Holland	Captain-Lieutenant, dead in 1720
Van Rosen	Denmark	Captain
Van Werden	Sweden (supposed)	Captain
Vaughan	England	Captain-Commodore, blown up in 1715
Waldron, John	England	Captain, dismissed 1713
Wessell, Hendrick	Norway	Captain, dismissed 1722
Villebois, Francis	France	Captain
Wilster	Denmark (supposed)	Vice-Admiral, but no flag appointed him
Wilsters (two)	Denmark (supposed)	One a Captain, the other a Captain-Lieutenant, Captain Wilster dead in 1724
Zotoff	Russia	Captain

XXXI. GENERAL LIST OF RUSSIAN SHIPS, 1710-1724.

A general list of the Tsar's ships of war in the Baltic from the earliest date to the commencement of the present year 1724, exclusive of the frigates, built and decayed, betwixt the time of this settlement at St. Petersburg and the year 1710.

Ships	Where built	Present State
Alexander, *pink*	St. Petersburg	Old and unfit for sea
Amsterdam, *galley*	Holland	
Arundel	England	
Astrakhan	St. Petersburg	
Bolingbroke	England	Taken in her passage 1714
Britannia	New England	Very old

[1] Of the 82 officers on this list, the names of 19 are given as of Russian nationality; 23 of British; 17 of Dano-Norwegian; 13 of Dutch; 5 of German; 2 of French; 2 of Swedish; and 1 of Flemish (Brabant).

Ships	Where built	Present State
Carlscroon Wapen	Sweden	Old, taken from the Swedes 1719
Cruiser	St. Petersburg	Broke up
Crown de Lieft	Holland	
Devonshire	Holland	
Diana	St. Petersburg	Broke up
Dumcraft	St. Petersburg	Broke up
Elias	St. Petersburg	Broke up
Fortune	England	Cast away at Revel 1717
Freedmaker	St. Petersburg	
Fredrikstadt	St. Petersburg	
Hangö Head	St. Petersburg	
Hobet	St. Petersburg	Broke up
Ingermanland	St. Petersburg	Repaired, but grown old and unfit for sea
Isaak Victoria	St. Petersburg	
Katharina	St. Petersburg	
Lansdowne	England	Very old
Le Firme	France	Taken by the English and sold to the Russians, rebuilt and launched in 1723
Leseta	St. Petersburg	Cast away in 1716
Lesnoy	St. Petersburg	
L'Espérance	Holland	
London	England	Cast away in 1719
Marlborough	Holland	
Moncure	St. Petersburg	Broke up
Moscow	St. Petersburg	Repaired, but grown old and unfit for sea
Narva	St. Petersburg	Blown up by lightning 1715
Natalia	St. Petersburg	Broke up
Neptunus	St. Petersburg	
New Kronslot	Holland	
Ny Stadt	Holland	Cast away in 1721
North Eagle (*Severnoi Oril*)	St. Petersburg	
Ormonde	England	Very old
Oxford	England	Broke up in England 1717
Pantaloon Victoria	St. Petersburg	Built by a Frenchman, but much complained of
Pearl	Holland	Rebuilt to the water's edge 1723
Pernau	Ladoga	Broke up
Portsmouth	Holland	Cast away 1719

Ships	Where built	Present State
Prince Eugene	Holland	
Princess	St. Petersburg	Cast away in the North Sea 1716
Randolph	England	Old
Revel	St. Petersburg	
Richmond	England	Very old, unfit for sea
Riga	St. Petersburg	Broke up
Royal Transport	England	Cast away in 1714
St. Alexander	St. Petersburg	
St. Antonio	Hamburg	Cast away at Revel 1717
St. Egudel	Archangel	Sold in Holland, broke up
St. Gabriel	Archangel	Broke up
St. Jacob	Holland	Rebuilt to the water's edge 1722
St. Michael	Archangel	Broke up
St. Nicholas	Hamburg	Broke up
St. Paul	Archangel	Broke up
St. Peter	Archangel	Broke up
St. Raphael	Archangel	Broke up
St. Salafiel	Archangel	Broke up
St. Varakiel	Archangel	Broke up
St. Uriel	Archangel	Sold in Holland and broke up
Samson	Holland	Rebuilt to the water's edge 1722
Slutelburg	St. Petersburg	Hauling up for rebuilding this winter
Standard	St. Petersburg	Broke up in 1723
St. Michael the 2	St. Petersburg	
Stora Phœnix	Sweden	
Viborg the 1st	Ladoga	Run upon a rock, and then burnt in 1723
Viborg the 2nd	St. Petersburg	Very old, unfit for sea
Victoria	Holland	Taken by the French, retaken by the English, sold to the Russians, and now old and unfit for sea
Wachtmeister	Sweden	Taken in 1719, old, and now made an hospital-ship

APPENDIX A.

THE SWEDISH NAVY IN PETER THE GREAT'S TIME.

WHEN Charles XII. in 1697 ascended the throne of Sweden, that country was in appearance one of the great naval powers of the world. Her navy had suffered heavy losses in the late war with Denmark; but these had been made good by Charles XI., who, in the latter part of his reign, paid much attention to naval affairs. Owing to the decline of both the French and the Dutch fleets in the last quarter of the seventeenth century, and to the doubtful condition of that of Spain, the Swedish navy was but little surpassed in numerical strength by any one of them; and it was only to the English that it was considerably inferior. A great part of its material was new. The sphere of action of the Swedish fleet lay almost entirely in the Baltic, or at any rate within the Skaggerack, and its officers and men had not the same experience of ocean-cruising as those of the other countries mentioned. Yet it had advantages which to a great extent compensated for this restriction of its experience. As an organised force it had a long history; and what in these days we should call its 'system of mobilisation' had been worked out in detail, and had been tested often. Why Sweden was in reality weaker on the sea than she seemed has been explained in the Introduction.

The Swedish war fleet, or Royal Navy, dates from Gustavus Vasa. He was its real founder, and its official continuity has been uninterrupted since he established it in 1522. A list of his son Erik's fleet in 1566 contains the names of seventy ships and vessels, of which fifty-two carried more than twenty guns, and twenty-three more than forty. Institutions introduced by Gustavus Vasa were expanded by Erik. The southern portion of the country, including the Kattegat coast, still belonged to Denmark, and Gustavus had been obliged at first to go abroad, not only for ships and stores, but also for some of his crews. In 1535 he established powder-mills, the number of which was increased by Erik, and ordered the registration of powder, swords, armour, and stuff for seamen's clothing. In 1540 he engaged the services of Venetian master-shipwrights, and was the first to have galleys built in the Baltic. Detailed arrangements were made for the supply of provisions by different districts, based on the local produce of the articles required; and where these could not be furnished the district was charged with the duty of providing the necessary carriage of the supplies. Gustavus promulgated in 1535 his Articles of War, with the object of introducing into his navy strict and uniform discipline, and economy in the expenditure of stores.

By the beginning of the seventeenth century, the naval policy of Gustavus Vasa and Erik not having been followed up, the Swedish navy had declined. In 1612, the year after Gustavus Adolphus became king, only twelve ships could be fitted out. The great king took early measures for the increase of his fleet. Certain *härad*, or 'hundreds,' were called upon to furnish artificers or building materials. By 1625 twenty-one new ships had been built and thirty galleys were ready for service. A scheme of Gustavus Adolphus, which was probably known to Peter the Great, may have suggested to the latter the establishment of the 'companies' mentioned on page 2, *note*. The former proposed to a meeting of delegates from the Swedish towns in 1629, that they should join in the formation of a Shipping Company, with the object of procuring and equipping sixteen ships which could be employed in the defence of the country, and in the trade and supply of the towns, being taken —as occasion required—on monthly freight. The directors of the company were to be inhabitants of the towns represented. Certain privileges were granted to it, and the seamen employed by it were to be freed from local imposts for six years.

The manning of his fleet also engaged the attention of Gustavus Adolphus. From early times an organisation for this purpose had existed in Sweden. Whilst the inland districts were divided into *härad* or 'hundreds,' which furnished their contingents to the land army, the coast districts were called *skeppslag*, a name which shows their connection with the naval force of the country. Irregularities in the methods of raising seamen had led to complaints from the inhabitants of certain places on the coast. To silence these complaints, an ordinance prescribing the proper methods of effecting the levy had been promulgated in January 1577, and made applicable to the whole kingdom. The Crown reserved to itself the right of calling out, in case of emergency, every one for the defence of the country, but in general undertook to 'raise' only a proportion of the coast peasantry, their hired servants, and the unemployed or vagabond population. Provision was made for the maintenance of the men levied for the service of the Crown. The organisation was further elaborated in 1602 by Charles IX., who made a beginning, as regards the sea service, of the *indelningsverk*, or plan of territorial distribution of liability to serve, which was modified some three-quarters of a century later by Charles XI.

Notwithstanding the existence of this organised plan of manning the navy, it was found necessary by Gustavus Adolphus, in 1616, to send for officers and men to Holland. Various ordinances were issued by him for the inscription and training of men for the fleet, the chief object of which was to regulate the proportionate numbers of the general levy, and also to have five companies, of 400 seamen each, ready for service when required. The result of these arrangements was that whereas the crews of the fleet numbered 4,210 in 1621, they had increased to 5,587 in 1630. Detailed pay lists were made out, and victualling accounts were regularly kept.

The administration of the Swedish navy was conducted on an organised and rather elaborate system. In 1594 the office of Admiral of the Kingdom was created. It was the duty of this dignitary so to attend to the shipyards at Stockholm and in Finland that some ships should be always kept equipped and ready for sea if required, and also to exercise supervision over the seamen. In 1614 an Admiral-Superintendent (*Holm-Amiral*) was appointed to the naval yard on an island in the port of Stockholm. He was specially charged with the care of ships in reserve and their stores. The regency during the early years of Christina's reign continued the work of Gustavus Adolphus. A Board of Admiralty (*Amiralitets-Kollegium*) was instituted in 1634. The seamen liable to service in the fleet were divided into three 'Admiralates' (*Amiralskap*) or regiments, each with a Vice-Admiral at its head, and certain provinces and towns were assigned to every Admiralate. A regiment contained five companies of 180 men each, of which four companies were to be of sailors and one of gunners.

The institution of a standing corps of seamen begun by Gustavus Adolphus, was completed after his death. This standing corps was 'inscribed' on a territorial basis in the coast districts of Sweden and Finland and in the Åland Islands. In 1638 three regiments of sailors and three companies of gunners for manning the fleet amounted, without counting officers, to 3,379 men. In 1644 the number had risen to 5,160. The fleet which put to sea in the autumn of 1675, comprised twenty-four ships of the line, also ten royal frigates, and twenty-four armed merchant vessels, and was manned by 2,981 marines and 7,181 seamen.

The war ended by the peace of Lund in 1679, had been disastrous for the Swedish navy. The ships had fallen in number to sixteen ships 'of the line,' four frigates, and six smaller vessels, not all in an efficient condition. The re-establishment of the national defences was now forced upon the attention of Charles XI. A standing army of 38,000 men of the *indelta* or territorial conscription was organised, besides 25,000 freely enlisted men in the outlying provinces. Special attention was devoted to the needs of the navy. Experience in war had proved that Stockholm was not a suitable place for the headquarters of the fleet. The harbour was too far from the open sea for sailing-ships to get away from it easily; and its waters were usually frozen over for several months of the year. In December 1679, Charles XI. announced his decision that the fleet should be laid up in the harbour at Trotsö, and that a town, to be named Karlskrona, should be founded there. A naval yard was laid out, with slips for the building of large ships, smithies, and storehouses. The first ship completed at Karlskrona was one of 76 guns launched in 1686.

Improved methods of raising an efficient *personnel* were devised ; officers were encouraged, in time of peace, to enter the service of foreign countries, to receive instruction in seamanship and naval gunnery. A series of decrees regulated the inscription and organisation of a large force, and seventeen companies of seamen were formed. They contained 3,172 men, besides a further number liable to be called out during war. Additions were made in the case of coast-towns, so that the arrangements introduced by Charles XI. resulted in providing for the manning of the fleet, 6,202 sailors of the general levy and 3,497 specially liable to be called out in time of war. Voluntary service was allowed for, the cost of pay and clothing for 1,200 volunteers being included in a year's accounts. Inducements, in the shape of good pay and free victualling during summer cruises and two-thirds pay in winter when on shore, were held out to merchant seamen, of whom 294, divided into three companies, were engaged. As a nursery for men-of-war's men, boys to the number of 100 were entered.

Special departments were organised or enlarged. The number of medical officers was increased : and both their pay, and that of officers of other civil branches of the service, were put on an established footing. A corps of pilots and a navigating staff had to a certain extent been recognised of old in Sweden. They were now formally regulated. The king's ships were to be piloted free, but a fixed list of pilotage fees for other vessels was drawn up. The cruises of men-of-war were largely coasting trips in the Baltic, and the peculiar formation of the Swedish coast rendered good pilotage a matter of the first importance. The duty of navigators—using the word in the technical naval sense—was principally that of piloting, and the 'steersmen' or quartermasters occupied the place afterwards assigned to the navigating branch of several navies.

The considerable naval force which Charles XI. bequeathed to his successor, was strengthened by the latter. Charles XII. added fourteen ships of the line, five frigates, and several smaller vessels to the fleet in existence when he came to the throne. He also strengthened the fortifications of Karlskrona, which had now become an important and well-equipped arsenal. The established or 'standing' *personnel* rose considerably. The territorial inscription gave in all 10,285 seamen. Besides these, there were a section of hired or freely enlisted men and boys, and a body of marines, in some cases volunteers from the land army; and also a company of gunners. The general result of the additions made to both *personnel* and *matériel*, was that in the earlier years of Charles XII.'s reign the fleet had fifty large ships with complements amounting to 18,000 men. By the end of his reign it may almost be said to have fallen into complete decay. (Geijer's 'History of Sweden,' French Translation, Paris, 1844; Bäckström's 'Svenska Flottans Historia,' Stockholm, 1884; Veibull, and Höjer, 'Sveriges Storhetstid från År 1611 till År 1718, Stockholm, 1881.)

The following lists (from Bäckström) will show the strength of the Swedish fleet at the beginning of the period to which the MS. now edited refers. It may be observed that the list on pp. 13, 14 of 'Navy Records Society,' vol. ix., contains the names of certain vessels not found in either of the following, which may have been hired from private owners.

LIST OF THE SWEDISH FLEET 1697.

Rate	Name	No. of guns	Built	
1st	Kung Carl (*King Charles*)	108	1694	Karlskrona, by Charles Sheldon
	Enighet-en (*Unity*)	94	1696	do. do.
	Drottning (*Queen*) Hedvig Eleonora	90	1683	Stockholm, by Robert Torner
	Drottning (*Queen*) Ulrika	80	1684	do. do.
	Prins Carl (*Prince Charles*)	76	1685	Kalmar, by G. Roth
2nd	Prinsessa Hedvig Sofia	80	1692	Karlskrona, by Francis Sheldon
	Prinsessan Ulrika	80	1684	Stockholm, by R. Torner
	Sverige (*Sweden*)	82	1678	do. do.

APPENDIX A

Rate	Name	No. of Guns	Built
	Göta (*Gothia*)	76	1686 Karlskrona, by Charles Sheldon
	Wenden (*Vandalia*)	82	1689 Kalmar, by G. Roth
	Småland	70	1679 Stockholm, by R. Torner
	Stockholm	68	1682 Kalmar, by G. Roth
	Karlskrona	70	1686 do. do.
	Victoria	70	1680 do. do.
	Bleking	70	1682 Karlskrona, do.
3rd	Wrangel	70	1662 Stockholm, by Mr. Fose
	Finland	64	1667 Bolkulla, by Mr. Doj
	Bohus	74	1663 do. do.
	Upland	70	1666 Lübeck
	Hercules	62	1650 Wismar, by P. Croswar
	Westmanland	62	1696 Karlskrona, by Charles Sheldon
4th	Södermanlund (*Sudermania*)	56	1693 do. do.
	Pommern (*Pomerania*)	56	1697 do. do.
	Öland	56	1681
	Halland	56	1682
	Estland (*Esthonia*)	56	1682 Riga, by Francis Sheldon
	Gotland	56	1682 Kalmar, by G. Roth
	Lifland (*Livonia*)	56	1682
	Ösel	56	1683 Riga, by — Tison
	Wachtmeister	56	1681 Riga, by Francis Sheldon
	Göteborg (*Gothenburg*)	50	1696
	Kalmar	46	
	Spes	46	1666
	Wismar	46	1694 Karlskrona
	Stettin	46	
5th	Riga	32	1684 Riga
	Stralsund	32	1688 Stralsund
	Stenbock-en	36	1678
6th	Falk-en (*Falcon*)	26	1688
	Fama	16	1678
	Neptunus	16	1687
	Jägar-en (*Chasseur*)	16	1686
	Svan (*Swan*)	16	1686

ADDITIONS TO THE SWEDISH FLEET BY CHARLES XII.

Class	Name	No. of guns	Built	
Ship of the line	Skåne (*Scania*)	68	1697	Karlskrona, by Charles Sheldon
	Prins Fredrik Vilhelm (*Prince Frederick William*)	50	1697	Window
	Wred-en	44	1697	Karlskrona, by J. Falck
	Fredrika Amalia	62	1698	Karlskrona, by Charles Sheldon
	Norrköping	44	1698	Karlskrona, by J. Falck
	Göta Lejon (*Lion*)	90	1702	Karlskrona, by Charles Sheldon
	Prins Karl Fredrik (*Prince Charles Frederick*)	72	1704	do. do.
	Brehmen	64	1705	do. do.
	Oland	60	1705	do. do.
	Tre Kronor (*Three Crowns*)	86	1706	do. do.
	Stockholm	68	1708	do. do.
	Verden	54	1708	do. do.
	Nya Riga (*New Riga*)	54	1708	do. do.
	Drottning Ulrika (*Queen*)	84	1709	do. do.
Frigates	Postilion	22	1701	do. do.
	Falk-en (*Falcon*)	26	1703	do. do.
	Reval	40	1704	do. do.
	Viborg	40	1707	do. do.
	Phœnix	44	1708	do. do.

It is to be noted that the date of building of every ship on the above list is prior to 1710, the year in which Peter the Great's Baltic fleet became an important force (see the first sentence of IV. p. 15).

APPENDIX B

ENGLISHMEN AND SCOTCHMEN IN THE SERVICE OF THE SWEDISH ADMIRALTY IN THE SEVENTEENTH AND EIGHTEENTH CENTURIES.

IN the lists in Appendix A the names of members of the Sheldon family frequently appear as builders of ships. In the Swedish naval history of the seventeenth and eighteenth centuries English or Scotch names are repeatedly encountered. In 1607 William Clerck (probably originally Clerke) arrived in Sweden in the capacity of captain in a troop of soldiers hired in Scotland on Swedish account. His son, Hans Clerck, became an admiral and had a son, also named Hans, who was born at Stockholm in 1639. In 1661 the latter was appointed gentleman-in-waiting at the Court, and was attached to the mission sent to England in that year. He entered the University of Oxford, and afterwards proceeded to that of Leyden. Whilst in Holland he received, in 1663, an appointment as lieutenant in the Swedish navy; but he first entered the Dutch service, and under Cornelius Tromp, Brakel, and Opdam, took part in campaigns against the English, Spanish, and Turks. On returning to Sweden he was made a captain in 1665, and in 1673 lieutenant-admiral. In the war with Denmark he commanded, in 1675, a squadron of the Swedish fleet. With his flag in the 72-gun ship Sol-en (*Sun*) he distinguished himself in the battle of May 26, 1676, with the Danes, and took command of the remains of the Swedish fleet after its defeat. He was created a baron in 1687, and died in April 1711.

Francis Sheldon, master-shipwright, was a relation of Gilbert Sheldon, Archbishop of Canterbury, and of Sir Joseph Sheldon, Lord Mayor of London. He is said, by Swedish biographers, to have joined in an unsuccessful attempt to free Charles I. from imprisonment. On the failure of this attempt Francis Sheldon took refuge in Sweden, where he was well received by Charles X. Gustavus, and was taken into the service of the Admiralty in 1655 as master-shipwright of the navy. He directed the building of several vessels; but, complaining that he had not been properly rewarded by the Crown, he left Sweden and returned to England in 1685.

His sons remained in Sweden. The elder, Francis John Sheldon, succeeded to the post held by his father, but died in 1692, when both his and his father's work was continued by his younger brother, Charles Sheldon, who died aged seventy-five in 1739. He had directed the building of not less than fifty-nine ships of war, some of them of great size for the period. He also proposed the 'old dock' at Karlskrona, which at the time was looked upon as the 'eighth wonder of the world,' and constructed various bridges and other engineering works. Bäckström considers that the beginning of scientific naval construction in Sweden is to be dated from the arrival there of Francis Sheldon, and that its continuance under his son Charles rendered the country independent of foreign teachers. Members of the Sheldon family continued in the Swedish service, maintaining the family credit in naval architecture.

The greatest English name in the service of the Swedish Admiralty is, however, to be found in the history of a later period. It is that of Frederick Henry Chapman, or af Chapman as he was called after being ennobled. He was the son of Thomas Chapman, a Yorkshireman, who emigrated to Sweden and became a captain in the navy, and afterwards 'major,' or chief of the staff of the squadron stationed at Gothenburg. F. H. Chapman was born at that town in 1721. His mother was Susanna Colson, daughter of a ship-builder in London. He studied naval architecture in Stockholm and visited England in 1741, remaining there three years. In 1757 he entered the service of the Swedish Admiralty as assistant master-shipwright at Karlskrona. He became principal master-shipwright—or, as we should say now, Director of naval construction—in 1764. He was probably the most celebrated naval architect who ever lived. His works on naval architecture long held their place as text-books of the art, and were translated into several foreign languages. He designed a large number of ships on principles which were generally and greatly admired and often copied. In 1772 he was ennobled. He lived to a great age, being nearly ninety when he died in 1808. (Bäckström, 'Svenska Flottans Historia,' 'Biografiskt Lexikon öfver Namnkunnige Svenske Män ').

APPENDIX C.

THE SWEDISH 'SKÅRGÅRDS-FLEET,' OR SPECIAL COAST-SERVICE FORCE

THERE is a brief allusion in the text to the ravages of the Russians on the coast of Sweden in the later years of the war which ended in 1721. These ravages were carried out with the deliberate intention of forcing the Swedish Government to make peace, negotiations for the conclusion of which had been in progress for a long time. The tactics adopted had an important effect upon Swedish naval history. An influential party in Sweden was convinced that the ordinary fleet (*örlogs-flotta*) was incapable of defending the coast from devastating attacks by an enemy's galleys, and consequently that it was necessary to have a special force for service in the *Skärgård*, or islet-studded series of inlets, which is the peculiar feature of Baltic hydrography. The later operations on land in both Finland and Sweden proper had been conducted near the coast: and the support of squadrons of small vessels by batteries erected on shore, and the movement of bodies of troops by water from one position to another, were common features of a campaign.

As has been already said, galleys had long formed part of the Swedish fleet: and the celebrated battle of Hangö-Head was essentially a galley action. In 1722, not long after the peace of Nystadt, a commission was appointed to formulate recommendations for the restoration of the Swedish navy and the improvement of its composition. This commission recommended that a *Skärgårds* fleet should be formed, and that it should consist of

6 24-gun *prahms*
6 18 do. do.
6 brigantines
30 galleys with 21 pairs of oars
40 do. do. 15 to 20 do.
70 *skär* boats

APPENDIX C

To make themselves acquainted with recent improvements in galley construction, officers were sent to the Mediterranean ports most famous for the building of vessels of the kind. The scheme proposed was modified at a later date, the numbers of certain classes of craft being altered, and some new classes being introduced. The modified plan, however, had not been fulfilled when another war with Russia broke out in 1741.

The experience of this war confirmed the advocates of a *Skärgård*, or separate coast-service flotilla, in their belief that it was necessary to the defence of the kingdom. It had not, however, been recommended that the flotilla in question should be anything but a part of the force administered by the Admiralty. It was not questioned that the peculiar features of the *Skärgård*—to the vicinity of which operations in war were likely to be confined—necessitated the employment of small vessels of special type: but it seems to have been no more supposed that these should cease to be under the naval authorities than it is now supposed that torpedo-boats or 'destroyers' should cease to be under them.

In 1747 the Diet resolved that Colonel Augustin Ehrensvärd of the Artillery should be directed to draw up a scheme for the improvement of the naval defences. Ehrensvärd belonged to the political party of the Hats, which was then in power in the Diet. In the proposals which he submitted, his leading idea was the necessity of supporting an army operating near the coast by a naval force. The inshore waters were inaccessible to both the army and the fleet, and it was of great importance that means should be available for transporting and landing troops in the enemy's rear. He therefore recommended the establishment of an armed flotilla, largely composed of galleys of light draught and large enough to ship a strong body of men. The new flotilla was to be in close connection with the army. It should, therefore, be separate from the navy, be incorporated with the army, and be called the ' Army's fleet ' (*arméns flotta*). The proposed force was to be put under the command of a general officer. An essential part of the scheme was the construction of a fortified port in Finland. Ehrensvärd's recommendations were adopted. He was promoted to major-general, and

L

given the command of his proposed fleet, a part of which was to be stationed at the newly founded fortress of Sveaborg.

Ehrensvärd, who was an influential member of the dominant political party, was enabled to force the adoption of his views of naval policy; not, indeed, without opposition, but for a long time without encountering effective obstruction. As he went on he increased his demands. He introduced into his fleet a great variety of craft, some of them essentially sea-going and very different from his originally proposed galleys. To man his fleet he required 22,300 soldiers, 5,862 seamen, and 300 volunteers. In addition to these, men were to be hired to act as shipkeepers. He was invested with the right of drawing upon the navy for the officers, petty officers, and dockyard officials, whom he found necessary.

Encouraged by the readiness with which his recommendations had been approved, he went further than perhaps he himself had intended at first. He maintained that the *skärgård* system should be extended to the whole of the Baltic. Even amongst his adherents he was held to have exaggerated the influence of coast operations on a land campaign. What he was now maintaining was really the negation of his own original recommendations. To extend the radius of action of his fleet till it reached the open sea, was to sever that connection between it and the army which he had laid down as essential. His case supplies a good illustration of the result of giving a specialist a free hand in dealing with the national defences.

In 1765 and 1766 the Caps—the party opposed to Ehrensvärd's—came into power. His views and procedure had recently been subjected to much unfavourable criticism; and his political opponents needed no great amount of persuasion to induce them to decide that the army's fleet was unnecessary, and should be abolished as a branch of the land forces. A *skärgårds* fleet was to be maintained, but on the former footing under the Admiralty, and in connection with the navy.

In 1769 the Hats once more became the most powerful party in the Diet. Ehrensvärd regained his former influence and effected the re-establishment of his army's fleet, at the head of which he was again placed. A separate galley-fleet under the Admiralty was, however, retained. The naval forces of Sweden were thus divided into three bodies —the war-fleet, the galley-fleet, and the army's fleet. In 1777 the galley-fleet disappeared as a separate organisation and was united with the army's fleet. The latter some years later was put under the naval department, though retaining much of its distinctive character. In 1803 it was finally made an integral part of the ordinary fleet. Changes of status and administration throughout three-quarters of a century did not materially affect the composition of that part of the Swedish naval force to which small craft belonged. Vessels and boats propelled by oars were used till a recent period, and even galleys were built as late as 1788.

APPENDIX D.

OFFICIAL DECLARATIONS OF NAVAL POLICY IN SWEDEN.

IN Swedish official documents of old date will be found certain expressions of opinion as to the value of naval defence, which bear an interesting resemblance, in the way in which they were formulated, to an often-quoted passage in the English Act of Parliament containing the Articles of War. In 1615 the Swedish Council of State, in complaining of the diminished naval strength of the kingdom, had used the expression: 'The fleet, on which the welfare of the whole kingdom seems to depend.'

The great statesman, Axel Oxenstjerna, who had always taken a special interest in the navy, addressed to the Council a memorandum, in which he urged that 'the fleet, which is Sweden's strength,' should be put in a thorough state of readiness.

The Introduction to the Articles of War of April 20, 1644, declares that they were promulgated 'for the defence, welfare, and security of the realm which, under God, depend on the country's fleet, a well-organised Admiralty, and good seamen.'

In 1766, after it had been decided to abandon Ehrensvärd's plans, the official proposals for strengthening the navy contained the statement that the fleet was 'the kingdom's most certain rampart, bulwark, and defence.'

APPENDIX E.

PAY OF THE ENGLISH NAVY IN THE AGE OF PETER THE GREAT.

To permit of a complete comparison being made between the pay of Peter the Great's navy and that of the English at the same date, the following lists have been extracted from contemporary documents.

In the year 1700 it was proposed that the 'pay' of officers in command should be increased—doubled in fact. The advantages which the proposal appeared to confer on the officers turned out to be considerably less than was expected, because though the 'pay' was raised, the allowances accompanying it were diminished. Much the same thing happened as late as 1861, when the practice of giving to officers in command of ships 'command money' was introduced. In individual cases the total emolument was reduced. These, however, were soon set right. In many cases the gift of 'command money,' as it was accompanied by a reduction of 'pay,' added very little to the previous remuneration.

In the 'Journal of the Royal United Service Institution,' June 25, 1880, Professor J. K. Laughton showed that about the year 1690 the pay of a captain of a First Rate was:

Pay	.	273*l*. 15*s*.
Table money	.	250*l*. 0*s*.
Servants	.	240*l*. 0*s*.
		763*l*. 15*s*.'

It would require a whole treatise to establish an effective comparison between the purchasing power of 763*l*. two hundred and nine years ago, and the purchasing power of the same sum now; but it would be no exaggeration to say that at the former date 763*l.* was looked upon as an ample income for men in positions which would now bring them in over 2,000*l.* To bring up an income of William III.'s reign to its equivalent in 1899, we should not go far wrong if we multiplied it by 3.

An Order in Council of April 18, 1700, contains a list of the proposed pay of naval officers. It was accompanied by a proposal for giving 'shore' or 'half pay' to flag officers, and to a certain number of captains, lieutenants and masters. The latter was a real boon, and largely made up for the reduction of the full pay, or, as it was then called, the 'whole pay.'

ORDER IN COUNCIL OF APRIL 18, 1700.

The whole pay	Now allowed £ s. d.	Proposed £ s. d.
Admiral of the Fleet	6 0 0	5 0 0
,, ,, White	4 0 0	3 10 0
,, ,, Blue	4 0 0	3 10 0
Vice-Admirals	3 0 0	2 10 0
Rear-Admirals	2 0 0	1 15 0
Captain to the Admiral of Fleet	2 0 0	1 15 0
Captain of 1st Rate	1 10 0	1 0 0
,, 2nd ,,	1 4 0	0 16 0
,, 3rd ,,	1 0 0	0 13 6
,, 4th ,,	0 15 0	0 10 0
,, 5th ,,	0 12 0	0 8 0
,, 6th ,,	0 10 6	0 6 0
Lieutenants, 1st and 2nd Rate	0 6 0	0 5 0
,, 3rd, 4th, 5th, and 6th Rate	0 5 0	0 4 0
Masters per month, 1st Rate	14 0 0	9 2 0
,, ,, 2nd ,,	12 12 0	8 8 0
,, ,, 3rd ,,	9 7 4	6 6 0
,, ,, 4th ,,	8 12 4	5 12 0
,, ,, 5th ,,	7 15 0	5 2 8
,, ,, 6th ,,	6 12 0	4 13 4

The establishment of servants was fixed as follows:

Servants to be allowed to
    The Lord High Admiral or General
        that commands the whole fleet . 50 men

Admirals of the White	. .	30 men
,, ,, Blue	. .	30 ,,
Vice-Admirals . .	. .	20 ,,
Rear-Admirals . .	. .	15 ,,
Captains . . .	.	4 servants to every 100 men in the ship's company.

The shore or half pay proposed was :

		Per Day.		
		£	s.	d.
Admiral of the Fleet	. . .	2	10	0
Admiral	.	1	15	0
Vice-Admiral . . .	. .	1	5	0
Rear-Admiral . . .	. .	0	17	6
50 { 20 Captains . . .	at	0	10	0
50 { 30 do. . .	,,	0	8	0
100 { 40 Lieutenants . .	,,	0	2	6
100 { 60 do. . .	,,	0	2	0
30 { 15 Masters . . .	,,	0	2	6
30 { 15 do. . .	,,	0	2	0

The new scale was not acceptable to the captains, and they appealed to Parliament to look into the matter. A pamphlet was printed called 'The Case of the Captains; humbly offer'd to the House of Commons' (1700). In this the difference between the old and the new emoluments was shown as follows :

CASE OF THE CAPTAINS OF HIS MAJESTY'S FLEET HUMBLY OFFER'D TO THE HOUSE OF COMMONS (1700).

	Per Month.		
	£	s.	d.
A Captain of a 1st Rate having 754 men allowed him ; his former pay was .	21	0	0
His allowance of servants being 1 to every 20 men is	33	6	0
Which amounts to . .	54	6	0
The double pay is	42	0	0
His servants now being 8, is . .	7	4	0
The allowance with double pay .	49	4	0

	Per Month.		
	£	s.	d.
A Captain of 2nd Rate's former pay having 640 men was	17	10	0
His allowance of servants being 32, comes to	27	16	0
Which comes to . .	45	6	0
The double pay is . . .	35	0	0
Servants now allowed being 8, is .	7	4	0
The allowance with pay doubled	42	4	0
A Captain of a 3rd Rate having 476 men; his former pay was	14	0	0
His allowance of servants being 23, comes to	20	0	0
Which is . . .	34	0	0
The double pay is	28	0	0
Servants now allowed being 6, comes to	5	8	0
The allowance with double pay .	33	8	0

NOTE.—The 'month' was 28 days.

It follows from the above that a Captain of a First Rate was to get, per lunar month, 49*l*. 4*s*. instead of 54*l*. 6*s*., a loss of about 66*l*. a year, equal to perhaps 200*l*. now. The Captain of a Second Rate got 42*l*. 4*s*. instead of 45*l*. 6*s*. The Captain of a Third Rate 33*l*. 8*s*. instead of 34*l*. a month, his loss being 7*l*. 16*s*. a year, perhaps equal to 25*l*. now.

The author of the pamphlet, however, does not say whether the proportion of servants which he gives as the old scale, viz. 5 per hundred men of the ship's company, was temporary and exceptional or not. The recognised proportion, at all events during many years, was 4 per hundred men. It is difficult to believe that the author deliberately made a misstatement which would have been discovered at once; and, evidently, he was not ignorant of the facts of the case. At the same time he does not explain why or when the long-established proportion was altered.

APPENDIX E

A full list of the pay as established in 1705 is appended. It is taken from a pamphlet, in the Library of the Royal United Service Institution, called

THE THREE ESTABLISHMENTS CONCERNING THE PAY OF THE SEA OFFICERS, London, 1705.

A TABLE OF THE MONTHLY WAGES.

Rank or Rating	Rate of Ship					
	1st	2nd	3rd	4th	5th	6th
	£ s. d.	£ s. d.	£ s. d.	£ s. d.	£ s. d.	£ s. d.
CAPTAIN *	42 0 0	33 0 0	28 0 0	21 0 0	16 16 0	14 0 0
LIEUTENANT	8 8 0	8 8 0	7 0 0	7 0 0	7 0 0	—
Master	14 0 0	12 12 0	9 7 4	8 12 4	7 15 0	6 12 0
Midshipman	2 5 0	2 0 0	1 17 6	1 13 9	1 10 0	1 10 0
Master's mate	3 6 0	3 0 0	2 16 2	2 7 10	2 2 0	2 2 0
Quartermaster	1 15 0	1 15 0	1 12 9	1 10 0	1 8 0	1 6 0
Quartermaster's mate	1 10 0	1 10 0	1 8 0	1 8 0	1 6 0	1 5 0
BOATSWAIN	4 0 0	3 10 0	3 0 0	2 10 0	2 5 0	2 0 0
Boatswain's mate	1 15 0	1 15 0	1 12 0	1 10 0	1 8 0	1 6 0
Yeoman of the sheets	1 12 0	1 10 0	1 8 0	1 8 0	1 6 0	—
Cockswain (sic)	1 12 0	1 10 0	1 8 0	1 8 0	1 6 0	—
GUNNER	4 0 0	3 10 0	3 0 0	2 10 0	2 5 0	2 0 0
Gunner's mate	1 15 0	1 15 0	1 12 0	1 10 0	1 8 0	1 6 0
Yeoman of the Powder Room	1 15 0	1 15 0	1 12 0	1 10 0	1 8 0	—
Quarter gunner	1 6 0	1 6 0	1 5 0	1 5 0	1 5 0	—
Armorer (sic)	1 5 0	1 5 0	1 5 0	1 5 0	—	—
Gunsmith	1 5 0	1 5 0	—	—	—	—
CARPENTER	4 0 0	3 10 0	3 0 0	2 10 0	2 5 0	2 0 0
Carpenter's mate	2 0 0	1 16 0	1 16 0	1 14 0	1 12 0	1 10 0
Carpenter's crew	1 6 0	1 6 0	1 5 0	1 5 0	1 5 0	1 5 0
PURSER	4 0 0	3 10 0	3 0 0	2 10 0	2 5 0	—
Steward	1 5 0	1 5 0	1 5 0	1 3 4	1 0 8	1 0 0
Steward's mate	1 0 8	1 0 8	1 0 8	1 0 8	—	—
Cook	1 5 0	1 5 0	1 5 0	1 5 0	1 5 0	1 4 0
SURGEON	5 0 0	5 0 0	5 0 0	5 0 0	5 0 0	5 0 0
Surgeon's mate	1 10 0	1 10 0	1 10 0	1 10 0	1 10 0	1 10 0
Corporal	1 15 0	1 12 0	1 10 0	1 10 0	1 8 0	1 6 0
Trumpeter	1 10 0	1 8 0	1 5 0	1 5 0	1 5 0	1 4 0
Captain's clerk	2 5 0	2 0 0	1 17 6	1 13 9	1 10 0	1 10 0
Able Seamen, &c.	1 4 0	1 4 0	1 4 0	1 4 0	1 4 0	1 4 0
Ordinary Seamen	0 19 0	0 19 0	0 19 0	0 19 0	0 19 0	0 19 0

* The allowance for servants is not included.
NOTE.—The 'month' was 28 days.

INDEX

Admiralty College, at St. Petersburg, 62 ; its members began to act, *ib.* ; functions of, 63
Antufiof, Captain, 92
Apraxin, Count, Captain, 64-5, 80
Apraxin, Frederick, Count, General Admiral, sits on a court-martial, 25 ; member of the Admiralty, 62 ; member of the Board for drawing up Articles of War, 74 ; character of, 77 ; is rather esteemed than beloved by the Tsar, 78-9 ; a humane man, 80-1 ; disputes with the Tsar in favour of Sievers, 85-6 ; mistrusts Gordon, 85 ; returns from the Caspian, 118. Mentioned : 5, 22, 42, 52, 65-7, 69, 76, 121-2
Armfelt, Swedish General, 21
Armitage, Captain, 92
Arseenoff, Captain, 57
Asof, capture of, 1 ; given back to the Turks, 14

Baggs, master block-maker, 6
Baker, Captain, 30, 48, 50
Baltic, the Tsar wants a port in the, 107
Barbarous ravages of the Russians, 49, 50, 81
Batting, Captain, 44, 52, 66
Bent (or Bents), Peter, master-builder and captain, 10, 13, 14, 44, 57-8, 62-3, 92
Bering, Vitus Jonassen, Captain, the famous discoverer, 25, 41, 44-5, 92, 128
Besemacher, Captain, 50
Block, Captain, 45 ; struck his pennant to the English Admiral, 46 ; was imprisoned and died of excessive drinking, *ib.*
Blorey, Captain, 55, 63
Brant (or Brants), Captain, 18, 30, 41, 92
Bredale, Captain, 30, 35-6, 41, 44-6, 50, 55, 58 ; Commodore, 88-9
Brown (or Browne), Richard, master-builder, 10, 17, 20, 100, 124
Bruce, Jacob Daniel, General, Russian plenipotentiary, 57
Buss, Count de, rear-admiral of the galleys, 19, 25 ; his ignorance, 22 ; his death, 43
Buturlin, Ivan Ivanovitz, General, 69

Captains, their pay and precedence, 119
Carabin, Captain, 89
Careybashes, timber vessels on the Ladoga Lake, 111
Chalks, one-masted flat-bottomed vessels on the Caspian, 3, 20
Chancellor, Richard, opened Russia to Western Europe, xi
Chapezan, Captain, 55, 66, 92
Chapman, Frederick Henry, master shipwright of Sweden, 142
Chapman, Thomas, captain in the Swedish navy, 142
Charles XI., reorganises the Swedish navy, xxii, 136-7 ; founds Karlskrona, *ib.*
Charles XII., the character of, fatal

to Sweden, xv; incapable of seeing that conditions had changed, *ib.*
Charnishoff, General, member of the Admiralty, 62
Clerck, Hans I., Swedish admiral, 141
Clerck, Hans II., Swedish lieutenant-admiral, 141
Clerck, William, a captain in the Swedish army, 141
Colmeroff, Captain, 89
Cooper, Mr., engaged for the Tsar's service, 120; quarrels with Gordon, 121; is not well received by the Tsar, *ib.*; in charge of naval stores, 125
Cosens, Richard, master-builder, 5, 100
Cramer, Captain, 28, 39, 50, 128
Cronenburg, Captain, sits on a court-martial, 26
Croyers, timber vessels on the Ladoga Lake, 111
Cruys, Vice-Admiral, enters the Russian service, 5; commands at Kronslot, 12; tried by court-martial, 25; sentenced to death, 26; the sentence changed to banishment, *ib.*; recalled and made vice-president of the College of Admiralty, 40, 62; memoir of, 40; admiral of the blue, 88. Mentioned: 5, 9, 17-19, 22, 24, 88, 96, 121

Danes in the Russian service, 5
Davenport, builder's assistant, 5; made master-builder, 62, 100
Deane, John, master-builder and captain, 5, 41, 44, 45, 48, 50, 53-5, 57, 64-5, 71
Delap, John, Lieutenant, 39; Captain, 65
Duffus, Lord, at St Petersburg, 92; superintendent of the yard, 92; rear-admiral, 120

Eckoff, Captain, 41, 45, 53
Edwards, Captain, 50

Ehrenskiöld, Nils, Swedish Admiral, 35-6; dangerously wounded, 37; carried to St Petersburg, 38; detained a prisoner till the peace, 35-8; is promoted, 38. Mentioned: 61, 84
Ehrensvärd, Augustin, Major-General, his scheme for the naval defences of Sweden, 145-6
English Fleet in the Baltic, 66-7
English merchant-ships convoyed by Russian men-of-war, 55
Englishmen in the Russian service, 5
Erik, King of Sweden, continues the naval policy of Gustavus Vasa, 133-4
Evers, one-masted vessels on the Caspian, 3, 117

Falkenberg, Captain, 92
Fasting, very hurtful to the fleet, 105
Ferguson, teacher of mathematics, 55
Fitch, Captain, 30
Flags, divisional for the galleys, 95; the Russian, 121
Fleet, Russian, for the Mediterranean, 108; or the Indies, *ib.*; in the Baltic, to be superior to the Swedes, 112; badly manned, 121
Flotilla on the Don, broken up, 14
Foreigners in the Russian service, 101; pay of, *ib.*; rarely permitted to depart, *ib.*; bad usage of, 117; engaged for the Tsar's service, 120

Galitzin, General, 69; commander of the army in Finland, 80
Galley fleet, despised by the officers of the men-of-war, 94-6
Gardiner, builder's assistant, 6
Golovin, Captain, Count, 66, 89
Golovin, Count Feodore, admiral of the fleet, 4
Golovin, Count Nicolas, 63-4
Golovin, Surveyor-General, 101

INDEX

Golovkin, Great Chancellor, Count, 67

Gordon, Thomas [Charnock's *Biog. Nav.* iii. 309], Commodore, 56; rear-admiral of the red, 61; Tsar's esteem for, 62, 90; member of the Board for drawing up Articles of War, 74; unfriendly relations between, and Sievers, 84-7; disparages Sievers to the Tsar, 84; is opposed by Apraxin, 85; had set his native country in a flame, 85; vice-admiral, 120; pay reduced, 126. Mentioned: 66, 68, 76, 87-8, 98

Gortz, Baron, Swedish diplomatist, 57

Gosler, member of the Board for drawing up Articles of War, 74; commodore, 88, 89; returns from the Caspian, 118

Gouter, Major-General of the Artillery, 75

Griese, Captain, 44

Guard-marines, eduction of, 56

Gustavus Adolphus, greatly increases the fleet, 134; organises the manning of the navy, 135; instituted a standing corps of seamen, 136

Gustavus Vasa, founder of the Swedish navy, 133-4

Gwyn, teacher of mathematics, 56

Hadley, builder's assistant, 5, 19; made master-builder, 62, 100

Hangö Head, defeat of the Swedes at, 34-8, 116, 144; banquet in honour of the battle of, 84

Harding, Mr., built the Royal Sovereign, 11; built several ships for the Tsar, *ib.*

Hay, Captain, 56, 92

Hollanders in the Russian service, 5

Hoogstraten, Captain, 92

Hutchisson, Captain, 44

Ismaiwitz, Commodore of the galleys, 36; rear-admiral, 43; vice-admiral, 88; a good soldier, 94-5

Jagosinski, Paul, Adjutant-General, 36

Johnston, builder's assistant, 6, 19

Kasheloff, Captain, 92

Kilkin, Alexander, execution of, 55

Kronslot, is settled, 10; fortified, 11; works at, 75

Lane, Captain, chief engineer at Kronslot, 66, 73; Commodore, directs the works at Kronslot, 90, 123; a sober, ingenious man, 93

Laurence, James, Captain, 83, 91

Lesley, General, 69

Lieutenants, are generally Russian, 102; ill-treat the warrant officers, 102; Russian, are worthless, 114

Lillie Swedish vice-admiral, 31

Lobanoff, Captain, 48, 57

Lopakin, Captain, 66, 80

Lotkeys, small vessels in the Baltic, 8; small galleys, 95

Lubrass, Major, an engineer, 25; makes the new canal, 123

Lybecker, George, Swedish general, leads a body of troops through Finland, 13; retires with precipitation, *ib.*

Masnoy, Captain, 89

Medals for victory at Hangö Head, 40

Menshikoff, Prince, 17; commodore, sits on a court-martial 25, 42; rear-admiral of the blue, 56, 60; of the white, 61; president of a court-martial, 72; vice-admiral of the white, 88

Mishecoff, Zacharia, Lieutenant, sits on a court-martial, 26; member of the Board for drawing up Articles of War, 74; captain, 83, 89

Muconoff, Captain, 50, 92

Nelson, Captain, sits on a court-martial, 26

Ney, Joseph, master-builder, 5, 100

INDEX

Nieroth, Colonel, commands the Swedish troops at Kronslot, 12; takes service with the Tsar, *ib.*

Norris, Sir John, commands an English fleet in the Baltic, 43, 46, 66, 76; entertains the Tsar and Tsarina, 43, 47; salutes the Tsar's flag, 48

Norroff, Colonel, member of the Admiralty, 62

Ofdyth, Gabriel, Russian shipbuilder, 101

Officers, Russian, lists of, 17, 22, 29, 34, 42, 49, 52, 60, 68, 87-8, 128-30; warrant, are not good in the Russian navy, 102; want of, 103

Ostergarn, taken by the Russians, 53

Oto, Commodore, Master of Naval Ordnance, member of the Board for drawing up Articles of War, 74

Oxenstjerna, Axel, takes a special interest in the Swedish navy, 148

Paddon, George [Charnock's *Biog. Nav.*, iii. 312], rear-admiral, 52, 54-5, 58, 60, 98; died, 61

Palsecoff, Philip, Russian shipbuilder, 101

Pay, of officers, 96-101; of officials, *ib.*; rates of Russian and British compared, 97; of ship-builders, 100; of foreign officers, 101; of Russians, 101; officers', deductions in, 126; of the English navy, 149

Perry, John, Captain, 6

Peter the Great, many of his reforms had been attempted before, xi; his municipal reforms, extensions of existing institutions, xii; his nautical procedure not without precedent, *ib.*; his foreign policy not a new departure, xiii; his predecessors had endeavoured to win access to the sea, *ib.*; his genius was pre-eminently practical, xiv; he discerned the secret of the Swedish Empire, xv; his immediate objective, the command of the Baltic, xvi; the first to conceive the possibility of making Russia a naval power, *ib.*; his early intention to have the Baltic, xviii; his visits to Holland and England, xix; ruthless in exterminating opponents, xx; not a doctrinaire, *ib.*; understood the laws of political physics, xxi, xxii; was a lover of shipping, 1; captures Asof, *ib.*; orders ships of war to be built, 2; builds ships on the Volga, 3; his travels, 4; quells the rebellion, *ib.*; captures a Swedish squadron at Kronslot, 7-9; resolves to build St. Petersburg, 9; makes a settlement on Kronslot, *ib.*; has some small vessels on Ladoga Lake, 11; favoured by the mistakes of the Swedish, 13; his disasters on the Pruth, 14; surrenders Asof, *ib.*; assumes the character of rear-admiral, 15; sits on a court-martial, 25, 29; addressed as rear-admiral when on board, 31; commands the fleet off Revel, 33; commands the Russian fleet at Hangö Head, 34-8; lands in a gale of wind, 39; advanced to the rank of vice-admiral, 40; commands the fleet, 58, 60; member of the Admiralty College, 62; builds the ship Lesnoy, 66; hoists his flag, 67; at the Hangö Head banquet, 84; disputes with Apraxin, 85-6; excuses himself to Apraxin as having been drunk, 86; tries to reconcile Sievers and Gordon, 87; made admiral of the red, 88; jealous of the reputation of his fleet, 115; returns from the Caspian, 118; claims an exemption from the Sound dues, 122. Referred to *passim*.

INDEX

Ramsey, made master-builder, 62, 100
Rays, Captain, 30
Rouble, value of, 99
Rue, Captain, 30
Rumanzoff, Adjutant-General, 71
Russian fleet in presence of Swedish, off Revel, 33
Russians, have an aversion to the sea, 102; failure of an attempt to educate, *ib.*; will fight well in smooth water, 114; their ships sail well, *ib.*; but are badly manned, 115; and badly manœuvred, *ib.*

Saunders, Commodore, 56, 59-60, 63, 68; rear-admiral, 87, 88-90, 98; pay reduced, 126
Savage, Jacob, Lieutenant, 119
Savage, James, Captain, 83, 91
Scampavias, small galleys, 95
Schafliroff, Baron, Vice-Chancellor, a converted Jew, 68
Scheltinga, Commodore, 17, 22, 24; tried by court-martial, 25; sentenced to serve as youngest captain, 27; restored, 27; commodore, 29, 32-4, 41, 46, 49, 52; rear-admiral of the red, 56; is paralytic, 57; death, of, 58
Schootes, timber vessels on the Ladoga Lake, 111
Seamen, Russian are not good, 102; great want of, 103; apt to forget their knowledge in the Baltic, 104; Russian, much afflicted with scurvy and vermin, *ib.*; their obstinacy in fasting, 105; are improved by success, *ib.*; necessity of finding employment for, 109; very few, in the fleet, 113; sea-sick, 116; inexperienced, *ib.*; employed in coasting trade, 117
Serocold, Captain-lieutenant in Russian service, 56
Sheldon, Charles, Swedish master shipwright, 142
Sheldon, Francis John, Swedish master shipwright, 142

Sheldon, Francis, Swedish master shipwright, 141-2
Ships, Russian, fitted with engines spouting liquid fire, and boarding bridges, 28; attempt to haul upon dry land, 74; causes many accidents, 75; Russian trade in Russian, 107; advantage to Russia, *ib.*; Russian, short-lived, 112; scheme for officering and manning, 112-13; want of able seamen for, 113; Russian, sail well, 114; are well provided, *ib.*; Russian, have never been in action, 116; to be sent up the Mediterranean, 118
Ships, Russian, lists of, 17, 19, 22, 29, 34, 42, 49, 52, 60, 68, 82, 87-8, 91, 127; general list of, 130-2
Ships, Swedish, list of, 138-40
Ships:—
Arundel, 30, 32, 48-9
Astrakhan, launched, 83
Bolingbroke, (52), 25
Britannia, 41
Cruiser, launched, 124
Devonshire, 45, 65, 71-2, 118
Diana (snow), 30, 32, 57-8, 66
Dumcraft, 18; condemned, 59
Egudel, 44, 45, 50, 55, 58, 65, 83; unfit for service, 91
Elias (snow frigate), 39; allows a small privateer to escape, 53-4; officers of, tried by court-martial, 54; captain and lieutenant of, cashiered, 54, 64
Espérance, 30, 52, 118
Firme, 30, 52; condemned, 59; rebuilt, 125
Fortune, 30, 34; wrecked, 51
Fredrikstadt, launched, 73, 76
Freedmaker, launched, 83
Gabriel, 39; condemned, 59
Hangö Head, launched, 61; tried, 76
Ingermanland, 44, 47, 73
Isaak Victoria, launched, 66, 67
Katharina (60), 20, 33, 38, 73; name changed to Viborg, 83

Ships (*cont.*) :—
Kronslot, New, 55, 66-7, 70-1, 118
Lansdowne, 24, 52, 55, 64-6
Lesela, 18 ; cast away, 50
Lesnoy, launched, 61, 66 ; weighed up, 73, 76
London, 41 ; wrecked, 71
Marlborough, 45
Moncure (snow), 21
Moscow, 44, 50, 73
Narva (60), 41 ; blown up in 1715, 124 ; weighed, *ib.*
Ormonde, 30, 55, 63, 119
Oxford, 24, 34, 44
Pearl, 30, 38, 44-5, 54-5, 57-9, 64, 66 ; rebuilt, 124
Pernau, 18 ; condemned, 59
Poltava (54), 20 ; allows a small privateer to escape, 53-4 ; officers of, tried by court-martial, 54 ; to be rebuilt, 72 ; rebuilt, 124
Portsmouth, 45, 53-4, 65 ; wrecked, 71
Prince Alexander, pink, launched, 51, 52, 54-5, 59, 64
Princess (snow), 32-3 ; lost, 50
Randolph, 24, 52, 57-8, 62-3
Revel, launched, 55
Richmond, 41 ; condemned, 59
Riga, 24
Royal Sovereign, 125
Royal Transport yacht, 44
Salafiel, 44, 46
Samson, bought in Holland, 17, 18, 30-1, 41, 44-5, 48, 50, 53-5, 57-9, 64, 66-7
Severnoi Oril (North Eagle), launched, 73, 76
Slutelburg, 41, 50, 52, 125
St. Alexander, launched, 55, 67
St. Andrea, launched, 89
St. Antonio, 24 ; wrecked, 51 ; hospital ship, 56
St. Jacob (frigate), 20, 57-8
St. Katharina, launched, 83
St. Michael, 30, 59 ; launched, 124

Ships (*cont.*) :—
St. Nicholas, 25 ; condemned, 59
St. Paul (frigate), 20, 30-1, 35, 38, 41, 44
St. Peter, launched, 89
St. Raphael, 30, 66
Standard, condemned, 55
Strafford, 24, 34, 44-6, 48 ; condemned, 124
Uriel, 44, 46, 55, 57-8, 65, 83
Varakiel, 44, 59, 66
Viborg, bilged and burnt, 24 ; another, formerly Katharina, 83
Victoria, condemned, 124
Victory, 24, 34, 50
Sievers, Peter, Captain, 22, 26 ; commodore, 27, 29, 34-5, 45, 47, 49, 52, 60 ; rear-admiral of the blue, 61, 67-8, 70, 76 ; account of, 61 ; favoured by Apraxin, 62 ; member of the Board for drawing up Articles of War, 74 ; unfriendly relations between, and Gordon, 84-7 ; vice-admiral, 88-9, 122 ; appointed to sit in the College, 90
Simpson, Andrew, Captain, 27-8, 30
Sinavin, Ivan, Lieutenant, 17, 28 ; captain, 41, 44 ; a sordid, drunken, ignorant fellow, 46 ; commodore, 88
Sinavin, Nahum, Captain, 44-5, 62-3, 65 ; commodore, 66, 68, 69, 88
Skärgårds fleet, the, 116, 144
Sklave, Fedorsee, Russian shipbuilder, 101
Slitehamn, Russians repulsed from, 53
Sparre, Count, Swedish admiral, 76
Stegman, Lieutenant, 58 ; captain, 66
St. Petersburg, building of, determined on, 9 ; the Tsar's determination to hold, 106 ; measures for the safety of, *ib.*
Strouds, flat vessels on the Volga, 110

INDEX

Stubbs, Captain, 92
Sweden, kings of, neglected the surest element of their power, xxii; the naval weakness of, under Charles XII., xxii
Swedes, essentially a maritime people, xxi; attack Kronslot, 12; are repulsed with great slaughter, 12
Swedish army, marches through Finland, 13; seized with panic, *ib.*
Swedish fleet in presence of Russian, off Revel, 33
Swedish squadron captured at Kronslot, 7-9

Thofft, Captain, 45
Timber for ship-building, 110; transport of, 111
Tobago, the Tsar's claim to, 108
Tonneshoff, Secretary of the Admiralty, 62
Trade, course of Russian, 107
Tressel, Captain, 64
Tressel, Rear-Admiral, his death, 40
Turnhoud, Captain, 57, 66

Urquhart, Captain, 56; killed, 71

Vandergun, Captain, tried by court-martial, 50-1; injustice towards, 51

Van Gent, Captain, 54
Van Hofft, Captain, 55, 57, 63-4; commodore, 68; rear-admiral, 88, 91
Van Merch, Prussian Privy Councillor, 65
Van Rosen, Captain, 92
Van Werden, Charles, enters the Tsar's service, 9; captain, 56; surveys the Caspian, 82; returns to the Caspian, 89
Vaughan, Captain, 30, 41
Vianen, Captain, 64
Villebois, Captain, 70, 80, 89
Volga, the, floods of, 110; navigation of, 111

Webb or Webby, builder, 6
Webb or Webby, Peter, builder, 41
Webhamey, Captain, 28
Wilster, Captain, 83, 92
Wilster, Vice-Admiral, enters the Tsar's service, 83
Wright, master mast-maker, 6

Yacht given to the Tsar by the King of Prussia, 58
Youths, Russian, apprenticed in England and Holland, 51

Zotoff, Conon, Lieutenant, sits on a court-martial, 26; captain, 65-6, 92; member of the Board for drawing up Articles of War, 74

THE NAVY RECORDS SOCIETY

PATRONS
H.R.H. THE DUKE OF SAXE-COBURG AND GOTHA, K.G., K.T., &c.
H.R.H. THE DUKE OF YORK, K.G., &c.

PRESIDENT
EARL SPENCER, K.G.

THE Council propose to include among the forthcoming volumes a collection of naval and nautical songs, ballads, broadsides, forebitters, shanties, &c., many of which—interesting reminiscences of the wars of last century and of the old navy of wood and canvas—live only in memory, and are fast dying out.

Such a work can only be carried out satisfactorily by the co-operation of many; what one has not, another has; what one has forgotten, another may remember; and an appeal is therefore made to the Members of the Society, and, through them, to their friends, and to all who take pleasure in fighting against the decaying influences of time, to send copies of any such verses (entire ballads or fragments—no fragments too small—with music when possible) as they may have or can write down from memory. It is hoped that in this way many pieces may yet be rescued from that oblivion which has already, it is to be feared, engulfed a great number.

The volume will be edited by Mr. Henry Newbolt (14 Old Square, Lincoln's Inn, London, W.C.) and Mr. C. H. Firth (33 Norham Road, Oxford), to whom, or to the Secretary, all contributions and suggestions may be sent.

May 1899.

www.ingramcontent.com/pod-product-compliance
Lightning Source LLC
Chambersburg PA
CBHW030434190426
43202CB00036B/213